of my
Son

On the Death of my Son

An Account of Life After Death

JASPER SWAIN

Edited by Noel Langley

THE AQUARIAN PRESS

First published by Turnstone Press 1974
This edition 1989

British Library Cataloguing in Publication Data

Swain, Jasper
   On the death of my son.
   1. Spiritualism
   I. Title   II. Langley, Noel
   133.9

   ISBN 0-85030-788-0

*The Aquarian Press is part of the Thorsons Publishing Group,
Wellingborough, Northamptonshire, NN8 2RQ, England*

Printed in Great Britain by Woolnough Bookbinding Limited,
Irthlingborough, Northamptonshire

10 9 8 7 6 5 4 3 2

Foreword

Down-to-earth may be an odd phrase to describe how a bereaved father found a means of communication with his dead son; but it was also true of the 'brother under the skin' to this book, *Phillip In Two Worlds* by Alice Gilbert — which, having been privately printed over twenty years ago, was necessarily confined to a more limited audience.

The reader who is venturing into this terrain for the first time will find the style clear and incisive: I make reference here to the teenage stenographer in the Los Angeles firm that xeroxed the author's original. She was utterly fascinated, never having read anything like it before, and 'hadn't been able to put it down'.

Jasper Swain practises law in the South African city of Pietermaritzburg. He had no practical belief in the psychic prior to his son's death, nor had he tried his hand at professional writing. His book is an unadorned account of what he experienced first hand.

The Republic of South Africa tends to condone a parochialism that often splits wide its white minority, itself divided roughly into ex-British Colonial and Dutch Afrikaner. The two groups delight in disagreeing almost anywhere on the compass, except with the fact that neither has anywhere else to go. From this standpoint, the country is a 'lonely long-distance runner' whose ultimate resolution must lie solely in its own hands.

In the old days of the country's Empire status, the most 'English' province was the Garden Colony of Natal, which occupies three luxuriant plateaus in the north-east. Durban flourishes at the semi-tropical sea level; Pietermaritzburg, once the government capital, dominates the first plateau; and this in turn makes way for the mighty Drakensberg mountain chain, which soars above the third plateau, eventually to give way to the high veld of the Orange Free State and the Transvaal. The national highway to Johannesburg of necessity follows the same route.

The average man-in-the street is easygoing and would like to be considered tolerant, but a bloody history of Zulu warfare has left him intractable to the idea of accepting the black man as an equal.

The cultural temper today is not unlike Western Europe between the two world wars; on the surface, confidently progressive; below, steeling itself against the twin bogeys of parlour-facism and racial emancipation.

I take something of a proprietary interest in the author, having lived the first twenty-two years of my life cheek by jowl, so to speak.

Jasper Swain is a man after my own heart. Since he first published his own indigenous version of his experience, he has been made to walk on tintacks in bare feet by the Poohbahs in his community.

I wholeheartedly concur with the philosophy contained in the book.

Bernard Shaw, when he was asked whether he thought there was life on the other planets, replied simply: "Of course there is! We are their lunatic asylum!" — a view so tolerant and sane that, again, I wholeheartedly concur.

Like the vulgar world at large, the occult byways swarm with factory rejects, gypsy tearoom fortune tellers, phoney gurus, bloated egos, and refugees from Manson's lunatic *gotterdammerrung*, but is it one of the few places where the Christ figure has not been subject to punitive distortions: and even if its more florid Tartuffes are as windblown as a judge in chambers, it is still the only unlocked door in the jail. We demean it at our peril.

Noel Langley, 1973.

We have not lost Mike. In spirit he is ever with us. And as a result of his passing as he did, we, all of us, have lost our terror of death.

That is why he asked me to write this book for him; in the hope that you, too, can draw comfort from the knowledge that death in this world is only a transition into a brighter field where we are infinitely better equipped to function.

The facts are presented as they happened.

I leave to you, the judgement and the blessing thereof.

Jasper Swain, Pietermaritzburg, 1973.

Part one

The day it all happened was in hot midsummer. It was just past noon, and the traffic was rumbling and roaring its way along the National highway. All of a sudden, under the small puffs of fleecy white cloud that hung motionless in the sky, tragedy struck.

Mike was driving his small green Mini back to Pietermaritzburg. The parents of his girl friend Moira had invited him to visit them in Johannesburg to watch the auto races at Kyalami, and on the Wednesday following, they had all set off back to Pietermaritzburg.

Mike had only recently sat for his school-leaving exams, and he was optimistic about his chances. His parents had even approached the University authorities in Durban, so anxious were they to see him take his degree in Architecture.

As he drove the little car along in the scorching heat, (the temperature was well over 102°), Mike's mind was focused on his future. He would now be leaving the comfortable home he had known all his life; but he was sure the University in Durban would soon enable him to stand on his own two feet.

Ahead of him, through the shimmering heat-haze, he could see the car that belonged to Moira's parents, Bill and Maureen. Bill was a careful driver who never travelled over 60 m.p.h. Riding in the same car were Moira and a friend of hers.

Until about an hour before the tragedy, Moira and her friend had been travelling with Mike in his Mini. But at Harrismith, Moira's eleven year old sister Heather decided that *she* wanted to ride with Mike. As Moira and her friend had become somewhat cramped in the little Mini, everyone was glad to let Heather travel with 'big brother' Mike.

They all agreed that when they reached Mooi River or

1

Estcourt, further down the highway, they would all stop again to allow Moira to resume her place beside Mike in the Mini.

They were all happy to be nearing the end of their long journey, for they had left Johannesburg early that morning and had been on the road ever since.

Bill, from the driver's seat of the big car, remarked on the heaviness of the traffic that day. Cars were continually passing them at 70 m.p.h., the maximum speed limit, and there was just as much traffic travelling in the opposite direction, towards the Transvaal.

Bill now noticed a late-model German car approaching, and remarked to Maureen: "Look, there's one of those new Duits buses." Idly he looked into the rear-view mirror to watch it disappear behind him.

Then his heart froze. He could no longer see the Mini. Instead; in a breathless, suspended second in the rear-view mirror; he saw the German car rear straight up into the air, spin end-over-end, and come down in a shattering cloud of dust.

He slammed on the brakes. How he managed to turn the car, he was never able to say, but the next moment he was racing back towards the engulfing cloud of dust.

At first he could not see the Mini. Then he thought he saw it pulled up on the side of the road. As he looked at it again, he realised that the colour was wrong. Mike's Mini was dark green. This Mini was pale green. Frantically he pulled the car to a stop at the side of the road, his wheels crunching and skidding on the loose gravel.

Away to his left, right off the road, he saw a battered dark green hulk. Two tousled fair heads lolled out of the left hand window. Without knowing it, he was out of his vehicle, rushing towards the Mini.

Maureen climbed out from her side of the car. She dimly knew that great tragedy had struck. As she ran towards the Mini, the figure of a man with arms outstretched materialised from nowhere, saying: "Don't go there, don't go there."

Calmly, icily, Maureen answered: "I must. They are mine."

When they reached the Mini, they stood aghast. Only the two rear wheels were still intact. Thence forward, there was nothing but mangled metal and twisted parts of the engine. It seemed impossible that anyone could have survived.

2

Bill placed his hand on Heather's head. It took him only one sickening moment to know his daughter was dead.

All he could say to his wife was: "She's gone."

Maureen, still unbelieving, said mechanically: "But Mike is only unconscious, Bill."

Bill ran to the other side of the car; through the tangled wreckage he slid his hand under Mike's shirt. Then he looked back at her and said numbly: "No, he's gone too."

Both of them stood there in silence. The world seemed to have come to a halt.

Then Maureen became aware of a choking noise behind her, and turned around. The other car was lying on its side. Beside it lay the twisted figure of a man. He coughed, then lay still.

Now other cars were stopping and people came towards them, wanting to be of help. Bill realised that Maureen could not be left there. Putting his arm around her, he led her back to their own car.

Then he went back to the Mini and tried to move the two bodies, trying to tear at the wreckage with his fingers to force it apart until he realised it was useless.

Personal belongings from the Mini were scattered all over the nearby road. Like an automaton, he began to pick them up and carry them to the boot of his own car. Forty-five yards down the road, he found the cinecamera Mike had used at Kyalami. The lid had been ripped off the case, but it was otherwise intact.

He also found a binocular case with the contents still intact. He then began to pick up the odds and ends Mike had left on the back seat of the Mini and transfer them, too, to his own car.

He kept watch on the Mini out of the corner of his eye, and now he saw a youngish man approach it and stop. Immediately a surge of anger flared within him, and he dashed back to the wreck to order him away. But the man said: "Can I help? I'm a doctor."

It brought Bill back to his senses. He asked the doctor to find out whether there was still life in the two youngsters. He knew there could be none, yet perhaps there might be a chance . . .

But the doctor made a brief examination, and told him: "They're both dead."

Bill vented his helpless fury on the onlookers, now

numbering well over a hundred. Mike had always carried his tools in the boot of the Mini, neatly wrapped in an old white blanket. Bill spilled out the tools and spread the blanket over the two tousled heads so that they were decently hidden from the public view.

Three policemen now arrived on the scene to prevent further collisions on the crowded highway. One of them came up to Bill, where he now stood by numbly, and told him they had already radioed to Ladysmith for an ambulance and a breakdown van.

A young couple on their way to Rhodesia with their children now came up to Bill, realising he was almost in shock. They offered to drive his womenfolk to the Colenso Hotel, where they could rest until Bill joined them, for he had refused pointblank to quit the scene of the accident until the two bodies had been given sanctuary.

An hour later, the ambulance and the breakdown van arrived and hydraulic jacks soon prised the wreckage apart. Only then could the two broken bodies be taken on stretchers to the ambulance, and only then did Bill allow his new friends to drive him to Colenso.

Maureen had already asked the proprietor of the Colenso Hotel to contact Mike's parents in Pietermaritzburg; and though a doctor had been summoned to Maureen and Moira, they had refused his help. They did not want to be under sedation when Mike's parents arrived.

Mike's father Jasper, a lawyer by profession, had begun that same day by pleading the cause of a drunken driver who had injured two people in a car accident, and he had worked hard, believing that the facts of the case warranted a touch of clemency.

As usual, came home for lunch at midday, and as usual, Clarice and Kevin were awaiting his arrival.

While they ate, they idly surmised that Mike would probably not arrive home before three that afternoon. They also discussed Mike's school-leaving exam results, which were due to be announced in the local press any day now.

Mike's younger brother Kevin, now sixteen, had been such a prize scholar that he had been able to catch up with his elder brother and matriculate a year ahead of him, so there was brisk sibling rivalry between the two. Where Mike had favoured architecture, Kevin had decided to practise medicine, and had already applied for admission to the University of Cape Town. At one fifteen, the phone rang. Amiably damning people who phone other people at mealtimes, Jasper answered the phone. He heard the long-distance operator saying: "Please hold on. Glencoe wants you," and idly wondered which of his clients would want to phone him at that time from Glencoe. Then he heard a man's voice ask for him personally. Jasper assured him that he was speaking. The voice then said: "I have a lady here who wishes to talk to you." Jasper heard Maureen at the other end of the phone.

"Hello, Maureen!" he greeted her pleasantly. "I'm glad you're all so close to home!"

Maureen answered: "Oh Jasper, there's been an accident."

Jasper replied: "Well, it can't be *too* bad. You sound as fit as a fiddle to me!"

She answered: "No, Jasper. Something tragic has happened. Mike has been killed in a car smash."

Jasper heard the words, but after that it seemed as if he had stepped out of his body and was watching himself talking on the phone. He said: "What was that?"

Maureen repeated: "Mike has been killed."

Mechanically he said: "And Moira?"

He understood Maureen to reply: "Yes," and then to add: "And Heather too."

With that, this man he was watching at the telephone threw back his head and gave a most terrible cry. "Stay there. I am coming," he told Maureen, and replaced the phone.

, He then saw this man turn around and become himself as he walked back to his wife. He looked at Clarice and said: "Mike and Moira and Heather have all been killed in a car smash."

Clarice just looked at him with wide open eyes, not wanting to understand. Kevin seemed paralysed. The three looked at each other for a long time. Then Jasper said to Clarice: "I will have to phone their family, and ours. Then we must go."

He decided to phone Clarice's parents first, but already he knew that he had no idea how to break the news to them. He decided only to report that there had been an accident, and that

5

he and Clarice and Kevin were leaving at once to find out what had actually happened.

Then he phoned his own parents, and listened to his mother's terrible cry of anguish when she heard the news.

In the long silence that followed, he replaced the receiver and went straight out to the car, where his wife and son were waiting for him. He filled the tank, and they set out for the Colenso Hotel.

Jasper now watched his 'other self' driving his car. It filled him with a sense of unreality, as though this person he watched was indeed another human being. Yet he could feel the strength of his own grip on the steering wheel. He could feel the touch of the accelerator as the car responded to his control.

Within himself, Jasper felt an icy, murderous anger grow as the enormity of what had happened became real to him. That Golden Boy he had nursed as a baby; the young hopeful he had taught to play cricket; the adolescent who often needed guidance, but took as little as he could . . . the flaxen-haired Grecian god, taller than Jasper himself, had been wiped out, obliterated.

Jasper was not a bad man. Hate, envy and greed did not have easy access to his heart; yet in that moment he resolved that whoever had dared to rob his son of life should be condemned to burn eternally in Hell. Mercilessly, implacably — pitiably — this bleak fixation built up in the heart of the man driving the car.

Not until they were climbing the mountains above Pietermaritzburg, did Jasper feel himself moving back behind his own steering wheel; and a bare moment later, he became aware of a radiant presence. When he turned his head to look at Clarice, he saw the golden form of his son sitting between them, and deep and clear in his mind came the words: "Don't do anything stupid, Jasper. Don't be a fool!"

Disbelieving, he looked away and then back at the image, only to find it gone; but a thunderclap was still re-echoing through his head. He knew quite clearly that it was the wish of his son that he overcame his rage.

He drove along, wondering why things had happened as they had. The urgency with which these horrors had piled one upon the other numbed him. It came upon him then that this must surely be the end of the road, so deep was the sense of desolation, the sheer and utter fear, that filled his aching heart.

At the start of that journey, Clarice had been as bemused as he, not knowing what to believe, not knowing what to think. Gradually she began to accept the fact that her eldest son was actually dead; and then the horror entered her mind that in his passing, he had suffered pain. "Please God, let him feel no more pain," she repeated silently as the car sped through the countryside.

Kevin, in the back seat of the car, was still unable to accept the fact that his only brother had been taken from him.

Only later was he to suffer the loneliness that becomes the constant companion of the bereft ... no more, the brotherly challenges and triumphs; no more the happy ribbing; no more arguments over pop singers and rock music ... only desolation now.

In the lounge of the Colenso Hotel, Bill and Maureen sat beside Moira, awaiting the arrival of Mike's family. There had been little or no conversation between them, for by now the shock had begun to work with a vengeance, and Maureen had retreated into a world where time no longer registered.

When the lights of Jasper's car approached from the road, Bill, who had been on the lookout, went outside to meet him. In silence they each put an arm around the other in a bond of mutual pity. Then Maureen came down the steps and joined them, and she and Clarice hugged each other, their grief too raw for spoken words.

They all went into the lounge before Jasper had had time to ask Bill what had happened. Now he saw Moira. Until that moment he had believed that both girls had been killed in the crash. Automatically he took her survival for granted, and his wearied mind waited expectantly for Mike to appear in the self-same lounge.

He soon understood that only Heather had died with Mike, and they all sat looking dumbly at each other. Then he realised that he would be called upon to identify the body of his son officially when Bill identified Heather. He insisted that he and Bill return to the scene of the accident. He knew he must see it with his own eyes. Only then could he proceed to Ladysmith, where the bodies of the two youngsters had been taken. Kevin was told to stay behind to comfort the womenfolk, and the two men drove back into the night.

At the Ladysmith police station they were told that because both youngsters had been certified dead on arrival, their bodies were already in the mortuary of the Government Hospital. The police sergeant, noticing that both the men were near to exhaustion, accompanied them the rest of the way.

Inside the mortuary was what appeared to be an oversize filing cabinet with much larger drawers than normal. When the attendant opened the top left-hand drawer, it stretched for a distance of nearly six feet.

There Jasper was confronted by his eldest son, familiar blond curls and stubbly little beard intact.

Jasper took one long look at him, noticing with relief the peaceful, relaxed expression on his face. He could not bring himself to lower the sheet in search of body injuries. There were none on the boy's face, neck or shoulders.

The drawer was then closed by the attendant, and the drawer beneath was pulled out. There lay the body of Heather.

There was no need for Bill to brace himself against the worst, for he had already seen his daughter when they lifted her from the Mini.

In dead silence the two men quietly turned and went out of the mortuary together.

Back in the car, the sergeant told them he was grateful to them for reporting in so soon, because it helped him in his duties; and he then wondered aloud how long it would be before the other body was officially identified.

Not until then did Jasper realise that the man driving the other car had also lost his life. For a moment the thought flickered in his mind that this was no more than his bitter due. Then he reminded himself that he had no knowledge, yet, as to how the accident had happened. And in any case it would be the hollowest of victories to allocate blame, when nothing could restore any of the victims to life.

They returned to the police station to find that no typist was available so late in the day; but as the certificates of death still had to be completed, Jasper sat down at the typewriter and typed out both affidavits with one finger.

8

They then returned to the Hotel at Colenso, and both the bereaved families left for Pietermaritzburg in their respective cars, arriving there at about eight that evening.

Jasper and Clarice proceeded to the home of her parents, where Clarice's father explained, or tried to explain, the divine logic behind the tragedy.

Next, they drove to Jasper's parents. Again they had to describe what had happened and confirm that Mike was dead. Jasper's father had called in the family doctor when his wife Louise had collapsed after hearing the news. The doctor had left sleeping pills for Jasper and Clarice, in case they were unable to sleep.

They drove home to find a car parked outside the house, and a young man approached them. A flare of weary anger in Jasper's heart subsided as the young man courteously expressed his sympathies. The tragedy had already been broadcast over the radio, and he wanted a photograph of Mike for the morning edition of the local paper.

Early the following morning, Jasper and Clarice opened their eyes to find Clarice's sister Rose and her husband standing at the foot of their bed.

Rose was younger than Clarice, and she knew better than anybody how close the bond had been between mother and son. They had driven up from Durban the night before, arriving at midnight to find the whole house still ablaze with light. When there was no reply to their knocking, they realized that everyone in the house had fallen asleep from sheer exhaustion, so they had slept on the living room sofa till sunrise.

When Jasper went downstairs to get the newspaper, the cold, hard facts of the tragedy were emblazoned across the front page, together with the photo of Mike.

At last Jasper accepted the fact that it had all actually happened, that it was not a bad dream; and when he had taken the newspaper up to Clarice, the harsh reality of the previous day finally came home to him.

He went to his office much earlier than usual, but his secretary was already there and knew all the facts of the tragedy. Jasper, having asked her to postpone his various cases, noticed a memo on his desk which ran as follows: "A Mrs.

Merrington has telephoned from Sezela on the South Coast with the following message: 'as you once helped her in life, she will now help you in death'."

His only response was indignation that a stranger should try to involve herself in his private grief, and he threw the memo into the waste basket.

Jasper had been brought up an orthodox Christian in the Anglican faith, but he had long ago felt that organised religion no longer played a realistic part in modern society. Over the years, he had investigated other religions — Lutheran; Catholic; Protestant — and even some of the more suspect beliefs which only appealed to minority groups. In none of them had he found any answers to his doubts.

He had even examined spiritualism, but that had also failed to satisfy him. He had then turned to the Eastern religions — Hinduism, Mahomedanism, Buddhism, Taoism and Zen — and was still unable to put his doubts at rest.

It was only when he came across the works of Paul Brunton that he began to detect a congenial philosophy. From there, he progressed to Vera Stanley Alder, and from her works to those of Alice Bailey, which he found too austere, requiring total application and discipline.

Therefore, when the tragedy struck, Jasper's grasp of spiritual values was still at the makeshift stage.

The undertaker Jasper contacted was also an old family friend, Sven Larsen. Although his assistant usually collected the bodies and brought them to the funeral parlour, Larsen himself drove the ambulance the hundred-odd miles to Ladysmith so that he could be present at the post-mortem, and he himself brought the bodies of the two youngsters back to Pietermaritzburg.

Sheaves of flowers began to arrive in an unending stream from friends anxious to express their sympathy and sorrow. Clarice was kept busy trying to find vases to contain them all.

Letters crowded out of the mail box that morning; messages of love, sympathy and support from people who were often nearly strangers. Among the first callers were the family doctor and his wife. He came both as a friend and as a physician, for he had treated Mike for all his various childhood ailments.

Clarice had been up before dawn. She had paced the upstairs verandah in the cold morning air, trying to create a pattern in her mind that might reveal some kind of reason for this tragedy. She also decided that the Reverend Tobias MacGregor should commit the mortal remains of Mike to the earth.

Mr. MacGregor had been ordained in an orthodox church, and he was besides a fine man whom Mike had deeply respected. The moment this thought took life in her mind, Clarice knew that this man could help her too.

She started enquiries as to his whereabouts, for he had left Pietermaritzburg some years before. Eventually a message was delivered to him; and MacGregor, without any hesitation, got into his car in Durban and travelled to their door to bring whatever comfort he could.

Dave and Brian, two close friends of Jasper, an electronics expert and a professor of music, had access to an organ and a large library of music, and between them composed a medley of church hymns and popular melodies Mike and Heather had most loved. A single church service was to be held prior to the cremation, as the parents had agreed that the youngsters' remains should be purified together.

MacGregor's first reaction was one of surprise, but he listened quietly to the whole tape, and then sat back quietly and said: "This is truly holy music. It is absolutely pure."

The stream of friends continued. Well over five hundred letters reached the family during the following week.

On Friday, Larsen telephoned to say that the two bodies were in his funeral chapel, and late that afternoon, Clarice, Jasper and Kevin went to view them.

As soon as they entered the chapel, all three had the feeling that it was warm and friendly and full of old friends, even though there was no one else present.

On Saturday morning, at the breakfast table, Jasper noticed that a fourth place had been set at the table. He went through into the kitchen and said to the cook: "Elphus, you know the *inkosaan* is no longer with us. There is no need to set a place for him. He will have no more meals with this family."

Elphus was a man forty years of age; a big, strong, strapping Zulu. The Zulus are brought up to believe that a man must never show his grief or sorrow, yet when Mike's name was mentioned, tears filled his eyes.

"Elphus, this was not said in reproach," Jasper assured him in concern. "This is a matter where the young *inkosaan* has been called by the Great One to join him in the skies. Our hearts may weep, but things are as they should be!"

Later that morning, when the various members of both families were beginning to arrive, Jasper went out aimlessly to water the front yard. The boss delivery man came up the driveway and placed two fresh bottles of milk on the ground. In a voice choked with emotion, he said: "*Hauw*! A terrible wound has been delivered to this house!"

Mike had always chosen his friends regardless of colour or creed, and now Jasper's heart went out to this old Zulu who stood with the tears streaming down his face. He said to him: "Mkize, the Great One came down to my home and decided that this young man would make him a very good leader, so He said to me that He wanted my son. As I am one of His tribesmen, I had to obey His request. I did not want to lose my son, but custom and law said I must."

This was completely in line with the beliefs of the Zulu people, and the old man understood immediately. His face brightened and he weighed his answer carefully. "Yes," he said. "I can see, when the Great One wants a thing that belongs to you, you must give it. Now the Great One has a very fine new leader indeed!" He picked up the empties and padded away, perfectly happy that what he had first regarded as a terrible injustice was, in fact, right and proper, as he understood things. Jasper's own sore heart derived equal comfort.

As he continued watering the garden, the delivery vans from the florists kept coming and going, and visitors kept arriving and departing. He moved to the furthest corner of the yard, so that these people, kind and well-meaning as they were, would no longer disturb his thoughts.

When MacGregor asked the two families where they wanted the funeral service to be conducted, Bill and Maureen chose Heather's church, and Clarice and Jasper had fallen in with their wishes.

However, five weddings had been pencilled in for that same afternoon, so MacGregor phoned Jasper and asked him whether the service could be moved to Mike's church; but when Jasper made enquiries, he found that his church too, was booked up that afternoon.

MacGregor then decided to take matters into his own hands. Having approached the Dean, he informed them that the Cathedral itself would be available at two-thirty that same afternoon.

MacGregor was an unusual type of man in this modern world; he was a true servant of God. Yet in his school days he had seldom if ever given a thought to his eventual calling, for he regarded parsons as a very distant adjunct to the society around him. After he had matriculated and gone to university, he went through a succession of temporary jobs, finding satisfaction in none of them, and finally he reverted to his earlier way of thinking by signing up as a school teacher.

For the next few years he 'stayed put' at a secondary school in Pietermaritzburg, and it was here that he came to know Mike. There was an immediate bond between the master and the boy. Mike would come home and tell them what a wonderful teacher he had, and it soon became evident to Clarice and Jasper that this was his first case of genuine hero-worship. MacGregor was one of the very few masters who really understand the minds of their pupils. But this period in the schoolroom also instilled in MacGregor a longing to dedicate himself permanently to the work of God, and eventually he went to the headmaster and tendered his resignation.

He then returned to the university and completed his honours degree in divinity, and then he proceeded overseas to take his diploma in theology in England, where he was at last ordained in Holy Orders.

On his return to South Africa he was appointed to a parish in Natal, where he soon endeared himself to his flock. One of his parishioners told Jasper that MacGregor had 'breathed the joy of worship' back into their services.

One day, a very troubled young woman came to see him. Having been a member of the parish for many years, she had, to her utter dismay, learned that her husband was having an affair with another woman. On the advice of her parents she had divorced him on the grounds of adultery. Then, after the divorce had been granted and the children awarded to her, she was told that no divorced woman could be admitted to Holy Communion.

MacGregor, convinced that the Church dare not forbid him to administer the sacrament to a woman such as this, took it on himself to admit her to his service with her newly-confirmed son. He also announced this decision from the pulpit, without mentioning her by name, and not one voice was raised in protest.

Unfortunately he then suffered a bout of flu and was obliged to take sick leave for three weeks. When this woman attended church as usual, to her consternation she was refused communion by the priest who was taking MacGregor's place.

When the affair was brought to the attention of the Bishop, MacGregor found himself on the carpet. He argued long and earnestly; his point being that the woman had obtained honourable redress according to the laws of the land: how could that debar her from the sacrament of communion? The Bishop understood MacGregor's point of view, but he was also concerned with upholding the rules and regulations. Nor was this the first time that MacGregor's 'attitudes' had collided with Church dogma. As he had administered to his growing congregation, so had he come more and more into collision with anything that did not actually 'feed and guide My flock.'

Confronted by conflict, MacGregor tried to resolve it as Christ would have done. Not by trying to put himself in the place of Christ; but by trying to do what he felt his Master would have approved.

It was increasingly apparent to him, however, that in the Bishop's eyes, he was not so much a pastor 'feeding and guiding My sheep', as an unsecular headache.

Violent rebellion began growing in his heart. All too well aware of his own shortcomings, he began to wonder which of his sins was the worst. Did he really merit wrath and censure? Must he be banished to another parish in his hour of bitter reckoning? He was fast trying to carry all the sins of the world on his own thin shoulders.

It was at this juncture that Mike had been killed and he answered the cry for help from Jasper and Clarice.

When he walked into their house, the first thing that he did was to pray for the two dead children; and to Clarice and Jasper, it was the most beautiful prayer that they had ever heard in their lives.

He talked to them both that night about the difference between their Personal Lord and the Lord of all Evolution; he described the laws of reason which decree the path of fate; and he prayed for their acceptance and understanding as he invoked the compassion of the Almighty in their name, so that their faith in His mercy should continue, even while they still felt they had been too roughly mauled at His hands.

After he had left, Clarice and Jasper felt a dim ray of sunshine penetrating the gloom that surrounded them; and they began the long, slow process of trusting in His will again.

Jasper did not want Mike and Heather's funeral to be an occasion for grief and lamentation. He wanted it to reflect them as they had been in life, carefree and joyous. MacGregor completely understood. He had never been able to understand why the flowers were taken off the altar at a Christian funeral; or why the Easter hymn was not included in the burial service.

He had conducted many funerals in his time; but now, as he sat down to write the oration, for the first time he found himself at a loss for words.

For the first time, he comprehended the enormity of what had happened. He knelt down and prayed to his Maker to give him strength in this wilderness of heartache.

While they were dressing for the funeral, Kevin came in to Jasper and said: "Dad, my only decent shoes are white and tan. They'd look crummy at a funeral!"

Like most youngsters of their age, Mike and Kevin had favoured the 'mod' type shoes; but now Jasper remembered that Mike had also sported more conservative footwear, so he said: "Go and look in Mike's cupboard. I'm sure his black formals will fit you."

"Dad!" Kevin protested. "Go in Mike's shoes to his own funeral?"

"Unless you're afraid he wouldn't approve!" answered Jasper with a straight face.

Relieved but still awed, Kevin went off to commandeer the shoes.

At a quarter past two, they drove to the Cathedral, where a large crowd had already gathered.

While Jasper parked the car, Clarice and Kevin went inside, unable to bear the sympathetic scrutiny of so many strange faces. Jasper quickly followed on their heels.

The Cathedral, built to hold a thousand people, was completely full. They took their seats in the front right-hand pew, and Rose and Mike sat beside them. At the front of the opposite row of pews sat Bill, Maureen, Moira and Maureen's mother.

MacGregor now approached the altar and genuflected, then slowly proceeded down the centre aisle to the main doors.

Larsen had drawn up the hearse outside this entrance. He now beckoned to the two groups of pallbearers to come forward. A step at a time the two coffins were brought down the aisle.

The small white coffin containing the body of Heather was carried by four members of Bill and Maureen's family.

Next came Jasper's brother Jake; then Kevin; then Clarice's four brothers, all bearing the coffin of Mike.

From deep within the heart of the Cathedral came soft music from the great organ.

As they drew level with Jasper, he saw that the coffins were being carried to the altar feet first. With a sickening jolt he recalled the time that a hospital orderly had pushed him feet first towards the operating theatre, to be sharply corrected by a passing doctor because 'only the dead go feet first'.

Now the two coffins were lifted onto trestles before the high altar, and MacGregor began the funeral service. Jasper and his family; Bill and his family; both were only dimly aware of the ritual of the service; but Jasper clearly remembered MacGregor saying: "Here was a young man without guile. I personally could not fault him. But we must not, we cannot, question the ways of our Father in Heaven. Christ could so easily have said: 'I am only thirty-three years of age. Leave me until I am sixty-six. I'll still save the world for You; but think of what *I* shall achieve meanwhile!' Death is only logical to a totally loving God. As mortals, we grieve deeply. But as Christians we can rejoice; for it was to children such as these that Jesus said, 'I go to prepare a place for you. If it were not so, I would have told you.' "

MacGregor's steady voice brought strength and comfort to the two bereaved families; and almost before he knew it, Jasper realized that the harrowing service was all but over. Soon the pallbearers resumed their burdens and began moving down the aisle towards the great doors.

Clarice took her father's arm. He was an old man of seventy-two who deeply felt the loss of this golden grandson.

Jasper walked behind the two of them. Then came Bill and Maureen, followed by the rest of their family.

Out in the bright sunshine the two coffins were placed gently in the hearse, and the final journey to the crematorium began.

Jasper had agreed that there would be no formal procession, as these were apt to slow down traffic.

But three motor cycle policemen unexpectedly converged on the funeral procession. With one rider ahead and two flanking the rear, sirens screaming, they conducted the mourners through the crowded business section of the town.

Jasper's eyes filled with tears as he realised the significance of this tribute to the cortege. It was not the habit of the local police to provide escorts for a private funeral; but Mike, who had owned a powerful Suzuki 250cc motor cycle, had become friendly with many of the traffic police in the town; and these off-duty men had 'booked themselves in' as their own private tribute. Just short of the crematorium, the motor cyclists peeled off to the left and stood at attention, saluting as the hearse came by.

Outside the main doors, there was a pause while the pallbearers re-assembled; then the two coffins were taken in and placed on the plinth, and the small crematorium was rapidly filled to overflowing with friends and sympathisers. Larsen, standing at the back of the Chapel, was alert to the heightened emotion everywhere. He knew that it would require only one person to break down, to plunge the whole assembly into tears.

Jasper remained outside, alone. He was touched to see such a crowd of youngsters, young men on buzzbikes, arriving at the crematorium in a never-ending drone.

At last he himself went inside. It was nearly time for the committal service. As he sat down, he heard the soft, soothing

17

music that had been selected for the tape. The Shadows playing "Marie Elaine" and "Stardust", the wonderful hymn "The Day thou Gavest", and Heather's favourite, "Once in Royal David's City", had all been combined into one harmonious whole.

As the music filled the ears of the congregation, Jasper could actually *see* the tension relax. When the music drew to a close, MacGregor took his place at the lectern, and having read the lesson, committed the remains. The service was ended.

But not until the congregation had filed out of the Chapel, did MacGregor kneel before the two coffins and let his tears flow unashamed.

Silently the families returned to their cars. As Jasper took one last look back at the crematorium, now yellow in the setting sun, the first wisp of smoke began twirling out of the tall vent-chimney. He knew it came from the varnish on the coffins. Heather and Mike were now committed to the purifying flames.

And at that same moment, far off at home, their pet Dachshund Mitzi lifted her muzzle and howled her sorrow to the skies. Then a deathly silence fell over the neighbourhood, not to be broken until the car carrying the family returned.

Part two

Jasper and Clarice felt that personal notes of appreciation should be sent to everyone who had expressed their sympathy. This was a task of real magnitude, and it occupied them solidly for the next few days.

No one in the family had ever met death head-on before, and to be visited by it so violently had forced it even further out of its frame of reference. But gradually an inarticulate resignation began to stir in their hearts. Bill, Maureen and Moira were frequent visitors to the house as each family drew comfort from the presence of the other.

Eventually Jasper remembered the note his secretary had left on his desk, the morning after the tragedy. He tried to push this niggling irritant out of his mind, but it soon grew to almost an obsession. Something kept repeating to him: "Go to Sezela, go to Sezela."

Finally he could ignore the constant pressure no longer and drove his car towards Durban, though he did not know exactly where Sezela was, except that it lay on the lower South Coast. At a filling station an hour or so later, he learned that the turn-off was not much farther ahead.

Sezela turned out to be a large sugar-mill, with its own estate surrounding it. He drove up to the main gate, where he found out that Mr. Merrington was one of the engineers there, and was told where he would find him.

Jasper had no sooner walked into his office, when the man greeted him with: "Ah you must be Jasper Swain. Mike told my wife to expect you here this morning. Not ten minutes ago, she phoned me to be on the look-out for you."

He led Jasper outside and pointed in the direction of his private house. Jasper, completely bewildered, followed his directions and was met by Mrs. Merrington on the front doorstep.

As soon as he saw her, he remembered having met her nine years earlier, when she had gone by another name. She had been abandoned with two small children, and was dependent on welfare organisations for assistance. Because Jasper often gave them voluntary help, her case had been referred to him. He had traced the errant husband to Rhodesia, and obtained a court order that forced him to support his wife and children. At the woman's request, Jasper had then conducted the divorce proceedings; she had subsequently met Mr. Merrington, a widower with three children, and married him. They were still very attached to each other.

As soon as she had invited Jasper into the sitting room, she sat back and placed her two hands over her eyes. When she next spoke, to his startled amazement, Jasper heard his dead son addressing him as 'Chud', a name that only Mike had ever used.

Because he steeled himself against the idea that Mike could still be living, Jasper deliberately set out to trap this imposter. Nevertheless he and Mike proceeded to discuss the fatal accident in detail; how it occurred, the cause of it, and the manner of Mike's passing.

At the end of an hour, Nina Merrington rubbed her eyes and came to herself, saying that she was over-tired and must rest. Jasper was too shaken to make small talk with her; but when he thanked her, he asked if he could bring Clarice and Kevin with him when he came back. She gladly assented.

Jasper drove the hundred miles back to Pietermaritzburg non-stop. The moment he arrived home, he told his wife: "Clarice, a miracle has happened! I want you both to come to Sezela right away!"

Clarice and Kevin were startled by his outburst, but all he would add was that he had contacted Mike, and he wanted them to talk to him too.

In his own mind, Jasper did not quite know whether he had gone off his head or not; but he asked them to keep completely open minds, and without further ado the three got into the car and went back to Sezela.

By now it was late afternoon. Again Nina put the backs of

her hands to her eyes; and Clarice and Kevin were able to talk to their beloved Mike.

After Clarice had asked all the questions her heart could hold, she was satisfied that this could only be Mike. He was so full of joy, so full of happiness.

Kevin too, after his own halting questions had been answered, was convinced that he could only be speaking to his brother.

When they asked him how the accident had happened, Mike said he would place Nina in the driver's seat, so that she could describe exactly how things had transpired.

She began by saying: 'He has placed me in a small green Mini car. It has a peculiar gear lever, a short stubby gear lever, next to my left leg.'' (The Mini had had its normal gear shift altered, and a remote control gear shift had been mounted between the seats.)

"It is a terribly hot day, and I am driving along a very crowded road. There is a little girl beside me. Her name is Heather. She is chatting to me about her mum and dad, who are in the car ahead of us. I can see their car, approximately fifty yards away. It is grey in colour; it looks like a Rambler. It is noon, and there is a mass of holiday traffic passing us in both directions.

"Now I see a black car coming towards us. As it approaches us, I see this other car coming behind it. I can see this other car clearly, because it is in the middle of the road, trying to pass the black car."

Nina paused a moment, and then said: "The sun is glaring on the windscreen of the black car, and reflecting back into my eyes. I can see nothing but a bright silver radiance. It is blinding me.

"*All of a sudden, the radiance changes from silver to gold. I am being lifted up in the air, out through the top of the car. I grab little Heather's hand. She too is being lifted up out of the car.*

"We have been lifted thirty feet above the Mini. And in one horrifying second, I see the little Mini and this large car collide head-on. There is a noise like the snapping of steel banjo strings. The little Mini bounces right off the highway, right over onto the gravel verge. It is finally brought to a halt in a cloud of dust when it hits a giant anthill.

"The large car is turning turtle in mid air. Its nose flips over until it is back to front. Then it smashes down onto the road on its side. Now it skids about four or five feet, and finally it comes to a halt with an ear-splitting crash. A storm of metallic dust is now glinting all over the road. The wheels of this car are still spinning aimlessly."

Nina stopped, obviously too agitated to continue.

What impressed her listeners was the fact that Mike had never seen the other vehicle *until after the silver light had changed to gold*. He and Heather had felt no sense of impact. They had suffered no pain. Just a gentle ascent into the air.

Nina recovered herself enough to continue: "Heather and I are still holding hands. We now descend beside the Mini. We see two crumpled bodies lying in it.

"We feel vaguely sorry that this thing should have happened to them. And we both fully understand that we are, now, so far as mortals are concerned, dead.

"We are also both aware that a lot of people have begun to gather round us. They are dressed in glorious colours. We recognise familiar faces; the faces of friends who passed beyond the earth before us. We are still hand in hand; now, guided by the one who first lifted us into the air, the two of us sweep towards the skies. We drift above the two round hills known as the Breasts of Sheba."

In heartfelt joy the three listened, transported by the fact that the passing had involved neither fear, shock, nor suffering.

Mike now addressed himself to his brother. Some time after the smash, Kevin had noticed that dust was gathering on the bike, and he had begun to clean it. In the process, he noticed that the drive chain was dry. In too much of a hurry to find the grease gun, he rashly decided to take a chance with the oil can. He bungled it however, and oil flowed out of the bottom of the casing and made a pool on the kitchen floor. Kevin had mopped up the oil with one of Mike's dusters, which he promptly washed and ironed before returning it to its ceremonial drawer.

Mike now informed him that he had watched the proceedings like a hawk, and warned his brother that if he ever made another mess like that, he would clip him over the ear!

This left Kevin devoid of further speech, because this episode had occurred long after the funeral and no one knew about it save himself. Yet Mike had not only seen everything *as* it happened, he was giving him 'a swift bounce' for good measure!

Mike next turned to his mother. "I am so glad you've begun to accept what has happened," he told her. "*Never allow yourself to mourn. When you do, it vitally depresses me in this world.* Send us your love, send us your happiness; these we can use in the service of our Father.

"The other morning, just after sunrise, you left the bedroom and went down to the garden in your dressing gown, and you picked a single, perfect white rose. I was with you then, and I surrounded you with my love. Mum, if you *do* get depressed again, go out into the garden and pick another flower. I shall be there with you again."

Jasper and Kevin knew nothing of this, having been asleep when Clarice had gone down into the garden. But in the weeks that followed, whenever Clarice went alone to the garden, Jasper and Kevin would notice that no matter how sombrely she would leave the house, she would come back later with her eyes sparkling and her face transformed.

Mike continued to his mother: "The only real bust-ups you and I got into were when you made me study half the night for those exams! I appreciate why you did it; but if we'd only known what was going to happen, there'd have been no need for you to take such a bloomin' great broomstick to me!"

Jasper, being the easy-going man he was, had always allowed Mike and Kevin to make their own rules at school, but Clarice knew that Mike was not particularly dedicated to heavy-weight studying, and she made it her business to keep his nose to the grindstone.

"Mike, where are you now?" Jasper asked him now.

The reply came instantly: "I am surrounded by the love and the peace of our Father, Chud."

"But *where* are you? What world are you in? Can you tell me?"

"I'm in a world that looks pretty much the same as your world, Dad; only there are different laws up here.

"When I say laws, I don't mean laws that govern the behaviour of the people here. I mean the laws that govern *thought.*"

"Mike, tell me more about that world. How do you get there? Where does it exist?"

"Dad, everyone comes here through the gates of death. You have to re-arrange your values to appreciate its virtues, though! While you are still on earth, you determine your own future in *this* world. While you are still on earth, your thought — your intentions — every thing you do — gives your soul a certain rate of vibration. For argument's sake, let's suppose your soul is vibrating in a fifty megacycle band. When you die and manifest here, you would go straight to the part of our world which vibrates at fifty megacycles. By the same token, if you're a slow-thinking sort of bloke who can only vibrate to fifteen megacycles, then you'll become part of this world in the fifteen megacycle range. It'll all depend on your rate of vibration, see?

"Therefore you yourself select the kind of scenery that will await you when you arrive here.

"The worlds above us are even richer in light and happiness. If I go up there (and I can) I find it too bright; the light hurts my eyes. And the vibrations are so refined that I can't respond to them! So I reverse gear and return to *this* world — which suits me just fine!

"The planes below this one are denser, dimmer planes. If I go down to them, it becomes murkier and murkier until it is so creepy that I scoot back here where I belong!"

"These worlds that you refer to, Mike — ?"

"Not so much worlds, Dad, as planes of existence. Though we have the sun and the skies and acres of beautiful flowers here, we don't have rain, as you people know it. Nor is there any blight to destroy the beauty of the trees. They look exactly the same as they do on earth. With one big difference, however. Here, they are all perfect. There are no high winds to warp and twist them. There are only gentle breezes. It is always beautifully coolish-warm, if you know what I mean.

"My greatest joy here is my sense of perfect freedom. We can go wherever we like, whenever we feel like it; this world is infinite.

"And though everyone you meet on this plane is at the same stage of development as yourself, he is still a rugged individualist in his own right; just as he was on your earth! Everyone has his own way of looking at things, and his own

24

way of speaking his mind! When you discuss anything here, you always learn something new, because the bloke you're talking to has such an original attitude. As I said, thought is all-powerful here. For example, if I want to own a brand new Jaguar, all I have to do is visualise the car in my mind, and it is created right there before my eyes, out of the thought-energy of this world!

"But we would think twice before doing that, because it means having to think in three dimensions! If I were to visualise the car as it looks in a magazine, that's exactly what I'd get! I need to think in terms of the width of the car, the interior of the car, all the fittings and where each rightly belongs. But Dad, the minute you think of it correctly, there it is! The difficulty is to concentrate *completely* on the *whole* car, exactly as it exists.

"If we are far away from one another and we want to make contact, telepathy is the accepted thing here. I merely have to think of the fellow I want to speak to, and bingo! he's right there! We contact each other as easily as you use the telephone . . . except that we don't need a phone!

"If someone wants to talk to you, you first hear him in your mind. If you want to go to him, you merely exert your will, and in two ticks you're right there! Takes a bit of getting used to, but it beats T.V. by a mile! You see how perfect everything is?

"This world is the right one for me at this stage of my development; but as my vibrations become more refined, I shall be able to visit the higher planes with ease. One day, I may even find that a higher plane suits me better than the one I'm in. We all progress this way. As we grow in spirit, we ascend to the next plane; the two processes work hand-in-glove.

"When you want to study the law and learn how it operates, you go to the Hall of Logic. There are many Halls of Knowledge and Wisdom here. You can go to any university you choose, though the lectures are all very informal; you discuss the subject with the lecturer, face to face. You can stay all day if you like; except that that could be forever, because we have no day or night here!

"We can travel from one end of this realm to the other as fast as lightning. Our bodies never get tired. Illness and sickness don't exist here. This is a world of perfection."

All this information took Jasper some considerable time to digest, and his next question was: "Mike, if you are safe in the infinite domain of God; where is Hell?"

This was met by a burst of hearty laughter.

"Gee, Dad," answered Mike, "I'm afraid there's no such place! My Father is a father of love and compassion. He can't, He would never, permit one of His souls to suffer; and Hell would be a place of suffering. I guess it only exists where you are now! Lovingly preserved in aspic by the sanctimonious.

"There is a more realistic law, in both our worlds, that has *just* as many teeth! *Don't try to identify white until you have learned how to identify black — and vice versa — because only then will you know what black and white are!* That is why you mortals were put on earth in the first place, Dad; to learn by trial and error. But because you *will* go by the letter of the law instead of the spirit of the law, you keep coming unstuck! Yet how often have you seen that same law in action, Dad, and sworn by its infallibility?

"When you and I used to talk together, you used to call it the law of the boomerang. But it isn't triggered by material cause and effect, it is triggered by the *intent* in your heart.

"For example, suppose you are driving a car too fast, and a little child suddenly rushes out into the road, and you knock her down; by *earth* law you would be frogmarched off to the nearest jail. But according to *divine* law, genuine remorse for having hurt the child can wipe the slate clean. If you didn't cold-bloodedly set out to hurt her what can you be punished for?

"Mind you, I shouldn't use the word 'punish'; the proper term is 'just desserts'. Who should understand that better than you? *You* taught me that 'as we sow, so shall we reap'! And from where I sit now, I can see that law operating twenty-four hours a day in your 'best of all possible worlds'! The only thing that puzzles me is why human beings still persist in denying its existence!

"There are no law courts here, by the way, Dad, because everyone of our laws operates within our hearts. Until we accept the fact that all negative thinking must always end in tears, we continue to create our own suffering. You'd be surprised how quickly I learned that the condition of my heart reflects the world around me! Now I would be willing to bet both our shirts, Dad, that the *really* real world, the *truly* true life, is here where I am. Your mortal world is more in the nature of a kindergarten where you and the other nut visit affliction on each other as a salutory lesson not to do it in the wiser worlds-to-come!

"The basic trouble is that most of you mortals will insist on *existing* rather than *living*. You trip over your frustrations until you can barely stumble from pillar to post. Why else do you think the eastern races use the lotus as a symbol of spiritual beauty? The lotus grows in the slime of stagnant swamps; but out of the muck rises the pure white blossom. Man eventually learns to distinguish beauty and truth from the misery and evil that surround him. And only from the acceptance of beauty and truth comes the wondrous return to the bosom of the Great One."

Jasper felt in his heart that Mike had beaten him to the solution of the enigma he called life. He had found happiness in the hereafter: not, in the pig latin of organised bigotry, damnation in Hell.

Indeed, Jasper took a very long time to absorb all that Mike had been telling him.

Obviously, when Jasper and Clarice had had time to mull over the meeting with Mike, they felt an urgent need to help Maureen and Bill as they themselves had been helped.

Alas, their two old friends appeared to take the news very lightly, and later Bill even took Jasper aside and said to him gently: "Look, Jasper, we don't want to hurt your feelings. You and Clarice are the closest friends we have. But you mustn't forget that you two have lost your eldest son, and you may be vulnerable to ideas that you would normally reject."

He also asked Jasper not to re-open the matter in the presence of Moira, as the idea of the dead still existing in a kind of spook side show could only increase her desolate sense of loss.

Jasper rather defensively advised Bill that he was needlessly depriving himself of much needed solace, but obediently promised never to mention the subject again.

Some weeks later, however, while he was functioning in a country court, he felt an overwhelming impulse to talk to Nina Merrington again. Unbeknownst to himself, he was becoming more responsive to Mike's vibrations, which now manifested as a warm golden glow in his heart.

He journeyed to Sezela as soon as he could, and during the session with Nina, he told Mike that Bill had chosen not to believe in his existence.

Mike laughed and replied: "Okay, Dad, it's over to me! I'll see that he gets a change of heart!"

Jasper, driving home later, had the somewhat superior feeling that if he himself had not been able to make Bill see sense, Mike could hardly do more from his golden plane. The thought had no sooner crossed his mind than he chuckled, realising the lack of faith he himself was indulging. Looking at it in that light, he could well understand Bill's feelings in the matter!

About four days later, a visibly agitated Bill suddenly appeared on Jasper's front doorstep. Clarice sat him down, gave him a pick-me-up, and asked him what had upset him.

"Last night," he began, "Maureen's sister came to spend the night with us. I realised that they would have a lot to say to one another, so I told her to bunk down with Maureen, and I would sleep in the spare room.

"That night I was lying in bed reading, when I suddenly became aware of a loud buffeting in the air all around me. At first I thought it must be caused by a sudden storm outside; it sounded as loud as a hurricane hurling itself at our foundations! But the noise was right there in the room! Except that the smoke from my cigarette in the ashtray kept curling straight up in the air, as if nothing was disturbing it.

"Then a terrific jolt shot me bolt upright, and I saw Mike grinning at me from the foot of the bed, large as life and twice as natural!"

Although Mike's lips did not move, Bill said that he heard him say: "So you thought I was six feet under, did you?"

Bill stared at Mike for a long time in horrified silence. Then, without any warning, Mike vanished and the room instantly returned to normal.

Bill was still so shaken by this outlandish encounter that he lay awake the rest of the night. Now he was calling on Clarice and Jasper to tell them that he was completely convinced that Mike had survived death; in which case his daughter must be just as 'alive and kicking' as Mike. He and Maureen had thrashed out the whole matter between them and now they, too, wished to meet Nina.

Nina welcomed them all with open arms, perfectly willing as usual to be of the fullest assistance.

Again she covered her eyes with the backs of her hands, and Bill and Maureen were quickly put in contact with their lost child. When Heather had assured them that her death had occurred exactly as Mike had described it, she set her mind to the problem of distributing her favourite posessions. She wanted her dresses and books to go to the children of Sunshine Home, a large hospital where children with TB histories were sent to recuperate. These children used to be taken on regular walks, and when they passed the house of Bill and Maureen, Heather had often stood on the verandah and watched them with sympathetic concern.

While they were chatting, Bill suddenly called out: "Hullo, Miss Muffet!" Heather responded instantly with: "Hullo, Jack Sprat!" Bill had used a greeting known only to the two of them: now he was completely satisfied that he could only be speaking to his baby.

Heather told them what she would like done with the rest of her treasures: her playmates were to get most of her toys, but she specified that Mr. Plod was to be awarded to her mother.

Jasper asked who Mr. Plod was, and Heather told him that it was a china duck that had been given her by Maureen and kept in a place of honour on her dressing table.

Then Heather turned back to Maureen. "Mummy," she said coaxingly, "I want Jessica to have my rag doll, even though it's not one of the expensive ones. Her daddy and mummy have all the money in the world, but they don't love one another the way me and you and daddy do." Heather was showing consummate skill in grasping the circumstances which shaped the character of her intimates. Now she requested that her golden St. Christopher medal — which had been left at home before the fatal trip — be worn always round her mother's neck. In conclusion, like Mike, she read the riot act to both her parents for making themselves so ill with needless grief. Then she allowed Mike to take the floor; and he cheered them all up with the news that they had freed Heather and himself from being earthbound; they would be free now to exert all their energies on the new plane which they inhabited.

Mike also asked Jasper to sell his motor cycle, promising that he himself would approve the new owner's credentials. For a start the bike would have to be properly cared for. He also promised that it would never harm a hair on the head of its new master, but he warned Jasper (who was inclined to want things when he wanted them) that this would take some time, and that it would be no use trying to speed things up.

Mike now addressed himself to Jasper, "You and Clarice have been wondering how to wangle a monument to us, haven't you?" he asked. "Well, don't lose any more sleep over it. You won't need to pawn the I.O.U.s in my savings account. Grandpa Vic will foot the bill, and the proper monument will be erected to me; one that I will view with great satisfaction." When Jasper asked him to be more explicit, all he would say was: "You'll learn about it at the right time."

As the five drove the long road home that evening, Jasper and Clarice, looking at the faces of Bill and Maureen, could see a serenity, an acceptance, and a content, which had not been there before. Talking to Heather had given them new courage and, more important, acceptance of the fact that their child had simply advanced to a new stage of development, while still remaining the same exuberant Heather she had been on earth. Now, whenever a spasm of loss re-awoke in their hearts, it was swiftly put to flight by the sure and certain proof of the continued existence of both children.

More and more often, Jasper and Mike ran into each other around the house. Mike looking as mortal as he had been the night he had appeared to Bill. On these occasions, Mike merely stood and looked silently at his father; but the perfect accord that flowed between them was something Jasper had to experience to believe.

Mike proved to be a first rate prophet. The cycle stood in a large dealer's window for over six months. All around it, daily, other cycles were sold, but never this cycle.

Months later, when Jasper finally blew his top to Mike, he received quite a shock. Mike told him that the cycle was to be given to Kevin, as soon as he was old enough to get a licence. "You see, Dad," he explained, "at long last you've accepted my death; now you can employ a logical attitude. You *can't* object!" Predicatably, Jasper did not object.

Some six weeks after the cremation, Larsen advised Clarice and Jasper that it was time the children's ashes were formally laid to rest, and at an appointed time the two families proceeded to the Columbarium for the committal of the ashes.

Jasper, Clarice and Kevin, the first to arrive, at once had the feeling that the hall was overflowing with people; people they could not see or hear, but who nevertheless emanated love and understanding in overflowing measure.

The service, conducted by MacGregor, was brief and simple, and although Jasper thought he had learned to live with the inevitable, the lowering of the caskets into the ground was a stark reality that drove home the terrible finality of the ritual with a vengeance.

Near the end of the ceremony, Clarice began to tremble from head to foot. Jasper held her by the arm, fearing that she was about to collapse. But Clarice continued to shudder until Larsen hid the two pathetic caskets from sight, and the small group finally walked away quietly and disconsolately.

At Mrs. Merrington's house, Clarice and Jasper talked to Mike again. When they began to discuss the funeral service, Mike said to his mother: "Mum, that sudden trembling you felt; that was Heather and me. I could see that the tensions were building up in you to a point where you were bound to collapse, so we gently supported you in our arms."

Jasper marvelled anew. None of the other mourners had noticed that Clarice was trembling. And only after he had taken her arm, had he realised how violently she was fighting against collapse.

Glen was not only the family physician, he was an old and intimate friend. From the first day of his local practice, Jasper and Clarice had been his patients, and a deep-rooted understanding had grown up between the family and the doctor.

Mike had told Jasper that Clarice should be completely checked over, because he felt that her blood pressure was too high, but at first Clarice had chosen to ignore the advice. Twice again Mike raised the matter with Jasper, and at last she agreed, unenthusiastically, to submit to a thorough examination by Glen. As soon as this had been done, she asked Glen whether there was anything seriously wrong. He answered "no", but prescribed three different types of medicine for her to take. When Clarice brought these home, Jasper realised that there had been good cause for Mike's insistence.

After six weeks she went back for a further check up, and finally, when everything had returned to normal, Glen admitted to her that he had been obliged to use the very strongest drugs to bring her back to normal.

Jasper knew the doctor to be a realistic man cast in a very conservative mould; nevertheless, he told him about the contact with Mike and Heather. Glen listened carefully enough and then professed himself unable to understand, though he accepted the fact that Jasper believed what he said. As a doctor, he was frequently present at the moment of death, and he confessed to Jasper that this moment of transition was usually preceded by a state of euphoria; an easing of pain and a subsiding into peace.

Although he did not pretend to assess the spirituality of what was happening, he could believe that Mike had been 'lifted up' at the time of his passing, and had experienced no shock or pain.

Finally the doctor said to Jasper: "The next time you talk to Mike, will you please put this question to him? I often think about it, and I have never yet been able to get a satisfactory answer. I treat many people in their final hours, and I have been obliged to prolong their lives as long as possible by using my professional skill. I repeatedly ask myself — is it right to prolong the lives of the old who are tired, and only want to die? When I use all the gimmicks that are available to me, I can prolong their lives by perhaps five or six days. Is this humane?"

In their next session, Jasper dutifully relayed the request to Mike, who answered on the instant:

"Dad, passing over from your world to ours can only be done with the consent of the person who is passing over.

"Two of the forces used to create a human being are the *immortal* soul and the *conscious personality*. The second is the birth-right of the person concerned, and while he lives, its word is law. It must give its consent before he can journey to any other world.

"A doctor may think he is prolonging the life of his patient, but he is not. What he *is* doing, is waiting for his patient to give the necessary consent to his own release. Believe me, Dad, *no* doctor can keep a person alive longer than the will of the Great One has ordained!"

This explained to Jasper why, in so many cases, old people could lapse into a coma, sometimes for weeks, before they finally passed over. Even if the body had no further need of life, the soul might not yet be ready to set in motion the complex procedures of incarnation. Jasper was beginning to accustom himself to the idea of a God who was both considerate and infinitely merciful.

As Mike had been so adamant that *only* by the consent of the person concerned, could the soul pass from this world to the next, Jasper now asked him whether this was also true of violent deaths such as his own.

Mike confirmed this: "Oh yes, Dad! My death was okayed well ahead of the accident! To be exact, on the previous Monday, while I was watching the races at Kyalami, I suddenly knew that my life was coming to an end, even though I did not know the *exact* moment. I didn't regret it, because I was also aware of the wonder, the love, and the beauty of the world that awaited me.

"Heather knew too. She was quite aware that the time was near. This is such a *wonderful* world, Dad. I wish I could describe the infinite beauty that surrounds us."

Jasper had only to reflect the joy Mike radiated, to know he was telling the truth.

Glen's mind was much eased when he learned that his efforts to prolong life were not contrary to nature; were not cruel, as his patients' relatives so often insisted. Knowing he was fulfilling a function both humane and logical, made him a much happier man.

Jasper reckoned once again that Mike had helped where help was most needed by the source that had asked it of him.

Because of the increasing number of sessions with Mike, various members of Clarice's large family of brothers and sisters had of necessity been brought into the picture; particularly Rose and her husband Michael, who had already been of such comfort and support to Jasper and Clarice.

Mike, who warmly approved of their generous help, said one day to Jasper: "Aunt Rose has developed a deadening of her fingertips, and her 'saw-bones' in Durban has diagnosed it as Reynard's disease. I want you to tell her that he's dead wrong. The numb fingertips come from trouble in her circulation; but plenty of the other local doctors are capable of diagnosing it correctly. One of them will, in fact, cure it."

When contacted by Jasper, Rose admitted that Mike was right. She and her husband were perturbed, for Reynard's disease had no cure: it merely progressed until it resulted in death.

Jasper at once suggested that she consult Glen; and after a thorough examination, Glen confirmed that the trouble lay in the part of the circulation that was triggered by the nervous system. He prescribed a remedy, and within a matter of weeks the condition began to show signs of clearing.

Mike also expressed a concern for the well-being of Clarice's father. Grandpa Mac was going on seventy-three, and he had already suffered two major heart attacks. The family had been unable to get a satisfactory diagnosis from his own doctor; he would only say that the old man's heart was so tired that it would gradually slow down until it finally ceased altogether.

Mac had been an engineer. Before his retirement he had been in charge of a very large chemical extraction plant during World War II. Because the output of the factory was strategically vital, he was obliged to remain on twenty-four hour duty. It was this repetition of long hours under constant stress that had played havoc with the old man's heart.

In his younger days, while studying for his Board of Trade papers at sea, he had been walking past one of the ship's large reciprocating engines just as a conrod snapped, and it had opened up a deep gash along his spine. He was laid up for a year, submitting to an endless series of operations on his back. He proved to be difficult to anaesthetise, so when the second operation came due, the anaesthetist said: "Well, it took long enough to put you out last time; you must be as strong as an ox. I'm going to make sure this time!" He then administered such an overdose of chloroform, that strychnine had to be injected directly into Mac's heart to revive him.

When the advancing years forced Mac to resign himself to the inevitability of death, he found himself on territory both alien and uncharted. No one was able to explain to him that everyone, sooner or later, crossed the selfsame threshold to eternity.

Happily for all concerned, Mrs. Merrington found herself in Pietermaritzburg on business, and Jasper was prompt to invite her to his home. He made sure that not only Grandpa and Grandma Mac, but Grandpa and Grandma Vic, would be present.

Mike came through loud and clear, addressing himself at once to his beloved grandfather. He described how Grandpa Mac's own mother was with him in the world of the spirit; and he described how contented she was. He also promised Grandpa Mac that he would describe the whole process of death to Jasper, so that Jasper could explain it to Mac at his leisure.

Jasper duly spent long hours with Grandpa Mac, with the result that the old man at last found a clear and charted path that he could follow. He was no longer afraid to face the so-called Grim Reaper, now that he knew what was going to happen, how it would happen, and what his part in it would be. A terrific burden was lifted from Mac's shoulders. Jasper had good cause to reflect on the virtues contained in the counsel of this golden son of his, this Golden Mike!

The time came when Grandpa Mac suffered another heart attack and had to be rushed to hospital. There it was soon evident that his passing was only a matter of hours.

One Friday evening, Mike came through and gently warned his mother that the time of passing was at hand; and he promised to be with Mac during the transition.

Early the following morning, Mac came out of his coma and fixed Jasper with his blue eyes, and said: "Mike is here with me."

"Is that what you were dreaming, Grandpa?" asked Jasper.

"No! It's *not* a dream! He's *here*!"

Three hours later, quietly and serenely, Mac slipped away from the land of the living — and as he did so, his lips were moving.

"Gee, Dad," said Mike a week later, "Grandpa was asking

questions when we fetched him here, and he hasn't stopped asking them yet!"

"Mike," said Jasper, during a session with Nina, "I think I am getting a much clearer picture of the laws that operate in your world. But can you tell me a bit more about yourself?"

"Well, Dad, there's quite a difference between the me that lives in *this* world, and the me that lived in *your* world! My body doesn't need food or drink to keep it going; nor does it need sleep to restore it.

"When you first arrive here, however, the routines of eating and drinking and sleeping are too firmly established to be eliminated at one fell swoop. So if you think you need to sleep, well, you lay down on a couch in one of the houses, and you sleep for as long as you want. If you think you need to eat, then you eat your fill. There are no excretory organs in our bodies. For example, when I drink a glass of water, it just diffuses itself throughout my system, and that's that! In other words, it's converted into energy. If I see a beautiful apple tree with bright red apples on it, I can reach up and pick one off and swallow it — all it does is to give me a tingling sense of satisfaction!

"We have hundreds of trees which bear fruit, and the fruit never drops off or rots. It stays crisp and fresh. When we occasionally feel depressed — and we *do* Dad; when the people we left behind are sorrowing for us too intensely, it depresses us up here! — the best way to cheer up is to wander out and pick an apple or a pear, or any other fruit we happen to fancy. It has the effect of recharging our batteries."

"What sort of clothes do you wear, Mike?"

"Any old thing we choose. It's simply a matter of concentrating on a particular cut of cloth and, hey presto! we're wearing it!

"There is one robe that we would never try to alter; our spirit robe. When we have public gatherings here, or when we call on one of the higher brethren in the halls of wisdom and learning, we simply discard our personal fashion of the moment, and our spirit robes appear at once. They hang in classical folds and come in an entire spectrum of glowing colours. We can never change the colour or alter the shape of a robe, because its function is to reflect the true condition of our spirit.

36

"Suppose, on earth, I had been a man with a violent temper. My robe here would have splotches of dark, muddy grey; or dirty red shot through with grey. This proclaims to all and sundry that it's high time the wearer began ridding himself of these blemishes.

"Most of us here wear our spirit clothing most of the time; when we combine this with our gift of telepathy, it's well nigh impossible for anyone to maintain a phoney front and hope to get away with it! No sooner have I *thought* a thing, than the person I'm talking to *hears* it. He knows exactly what's making me tick!

"As no dust or grime exists up here, we have no reason to wash our clothes. Nor do we need dry-cleaners. When we feel that our clothes don't have the shine we'd like them to have, we exercise our minds, and the clothes shine as brightly as we deserve.

"We have a lot of fun with the teenagers who have just arrived here. Especially the girls, when they think they're still the cat's whiskers. Oh, Dad, you'd laugh to see them primping around as if they were in a department store, changing out of one set of glad rags to put on another, and then starting again from scratch and dreaming up something even more weird and wonderful! Which promptly appears, as large as life and twice as natural! They have the time of their lives for hours!"

Jasper was fascinated by the idea of *thought manifesting as matter;* and he asked Mike to elaborate further.

"Well," said Mike, happy to oblige, "our Father is the creator of this entire magnificent cosmos and its untold galaxies. The galaxies are comprised of universal systems, millions and millions in number. We are the sons of this same Father — believe me, we are! — and we too, like Him, must one day become creators; which is why we are allowed to practise when and however we want to.

"This plane where I exist now, like all the nearby planes, is *infinite* in concept. We never need to jostle everybody out of the way, to grab the best place in the queue. Some of us like to live in communities, others like to live in rural cottages on the rolling downs, or even alone in the forests. We are free to choose *where* we would like to live, and *with whom* we would like to live.

"Our particular place in creation is distinguished by the way it reflects the law of retribution. When I move down to our lower planes, I see people getting up to the most idiotic shenanigans. For example, I saw this one bloke surrounded by piles and piles of gold; he was literally buried under it! Yet he kept jealously counting every coin. He didn't even pause to look up when I greeted him; he just grunted and kept on counting. I thought that this miser was nuts to sit there counting his money as if he could still buy wealth and importance with it. So I asked one of the elder brothers about him, because they are always approachable when we go to them with a problem that is perplexing us. The elder explained that on earth, this bloke had been an honest-to-goodness miser. Every night, when all his doors were locked and his curtains drawn, he used to haul out his gold and count it until he was cross-eyed with fatigue.

"When he passed over, he was still the same man he had been on earth, of course, so he got so homesick for the gold he had left behind, that finally piles of it appeared all round him! Thought had become fact; as it always does on this plane. Well, there the gold *was*; so he sat down to count it as he had never counted it before! Then he discovered that just by thinking, he could turn it into twice the size it was before. He must have been sitting there for over thirty years of earth time, just multiplying his wealth. And he'll be perfectly happy doing just that — until he eventually realises that gold is utterly useless to him here. We have no wealth or poverty here. And so it will finally dawn on him that he has been wasting his time. And no one will regret it more than the poor old bloke himself!

"And there was this other fellow who had been a drunkard all his earthly life; when he passed over here, he began with a rabid desire to drink a whole case of good brandy. So, lo and behold, a case of brandy appeared under his nose! He pried open the lid, grabbed the nearest bottle by its neck, and drank it at one gulp. It tasted exactly like it had on earth; but here comes the snag, Dad; he couldn't get drunk! You see, in order to get drunk, he would have to *imagine* himself drunk! But because his mind was now one with its creator, it refused to make itself drunk! Drink had only been an alibi on earth; a device to avoid facing reality; so when he drank to avoid facing reality *here*, he realised at long last that no matter how much booze he poured down his gullet, it had left him stone cold sober!

"What worse punishment could befall a miser or a drunk who had abused the fruits of the earth? But the beauty is that *they themselves determined their own punishments.* There is no Great Judge presiding over us here, handing out dry bread and water and solitary confinement! When a new soul comes to us there is no vindictive Confessor who says: 'You have been good, go to Heaven!' or: 'You have been bad, go to Hell!' and then hurls you into the fiery pit anyway!

"Again I tell you that our Father is one of infinite love and compassion. Any punishment brought about in your world, *but accountable in ours,* is paid for solely by the transgressor himself.

"Conservation of energy is a prime law here. That really means moderation. We learn to be moderate in all things. The miser allowed his sense of balance to turn turtle because he lusted for gold and nothing but gold. The drunkard was so afraid to face life that he drank himself into insensibility, instead of using his alcohol as a reasonable pick-me-up at the end of a hard day's work."

Jasper asked Mike how he occupied himself in the Golden World, in view of the fact that he had set his heart on architecture in his earth life. Did architecture come into the picture at all?

"You can bet your boots!" answered Mike. "Once a fellow reaches *this* stage in his development, he's bound to apply critical taste to the kind of place he wants to live in. As soon as I arrived here, I was shown the sights by Uncle Mark. People who practised architecture on earth because they loved the profession, like he did, inevitably seek out their own kind and put out the 'business as usual' sign here.

"When a new boy like me is ready to shop for a home of his own, he 'makes his number' with these architectural types, and we all sit down and discuss what kind of house would suit me best.

"Remember we never have rain or bad weather, so there are no wear-and-tear problems. As a matter of fact, there's no need for a house at all! But if you *want* a house, you sort of pick and choose until gradually you decide on such-and-such a house with so many rooms. If you want ten thousand rooms, you can have ten thousand rooms, though it seems a bit unnecessary. It would be a great big echoing white elephant, in case you hadn't banked on that!

"At any rate, as soon as you've decided on the kind of house you want, you look for the perfect site. There are valleys, mountains, rivers, even oceans in our world; so you start cruising about a hundred and fifty feet above the ground, at a fair speed, say two hundred miles an hour — until you find the spot that tickles your fancy.

"I wanted mine to be somewhere near a congenial community, and I saw exactly what the doctor ordered. It was perched on a gentle slope, protected by beautiful trees and springy green turf. The grass grows to about three inches high here, and it's beautifully soft to walk on. It never needs cutting; it never withers; it always remains this beautiful emerald green.

"Once I had picked my site, Mark called in the architects. They sat down and visualised, in their minds, the type of house that would suit me best. Then the builders arrived. There were three of them, and they sat down right beside the architects.

"A minute later, right there on the plot I had selected, the shimmering outlines of my house began to appear! Then everybody looked at me, and Mark said: 'Well, Mike? Is that more or less what you had in mind?'

"I can't tell you how excited it felt to be a *bona fide* home owner! I hollered back 'You bet it is!' and at once the transparent shell started to take on a solid form. In twenty minutes, there was my house!

"It is perfect in every detail, Dad! Somehow or other, the various bods had read my mind; every trick of the trade I had ever envied from afar has been incorporated into this brand new home of mine.

"I took possession that very same hour and sent out mental invitations to all my friends to attend the housewarming. In no time flat they were all there in person, and I welcomed each one at my own front door! The first item on the agenda was to ask one of the elders to join us. We sat round him in a circle and conveyed our gratitude and joy to the Great One. After which, we had a pop concert! Yes, Dad! We used every kind of music —

you know how fond of rock and roll I used to be on earth —
well we soon had a full-scale orchestra going strong, and we
really did ourselves proud! It was a fantastic housewarming!

"It soon became obvious that the house wasn't big enough to
hold us all, so I sent out an S.O.S. to the original architects.
And as soon as we all put our heads together in a
sit-down-and-think session, lo and behold, the house increased
to the exact capacity we needed!

"Believe me, Dad, this universal sharing of everything has to
be seen to be believed. There is no envy, there is no greed; there
is no: 'You've got more than I have', because the minute you
want anything, it's there!

"You remember how I loved to walk in the rain in nothing
but a singlet and a pair of shorts, when I was a nipper? Well,
whenever I need to feel the refreshing rain beating in my face,
and the wind blowing my head clear, I go out into an open field
and I *think* — and then I enjoy my own private thunderstorm!
It doesn't interfere with anyone else; I take good care that it
doesn't; we make a point of live-and-let-live on this plane!

"The rain forms little puddles as I walk; yet when I turn
round and look behind me, there's no sign of it — only the usual
long green grass. It takes some getting used to, the fact that the
mind is a creative weapon!

"I used the wrong word there," he added, and thought it
over. "Not weapon. 'Instrument' is a much nicer way of saying
it."

"But Mike," Jasper enquired, "what are you allowed to do if
any of your neighbours turn out to be neither kind nor
considerate?"

"That couldn't happen here. We're all at the same stage of
development. If one of us were to disturb the harmony, even
unintentionally, one of the elders would nip along smartly and
nudge him back into line. Sometimes the best of us are apt to
slip up, of course. That's when the elders point out the error of
our ways, and we correct ourselves at once.

"It is so serene here that one is immediately remorseful for
having been the 'odd man out'; and the remorse immediately
rights the wrong.

"No one is ever punished in this world. A man punishes
himself if he has broken the rules of happy living."

When Mike warned that one of Clarice's brothers, Rich, was working himself into such a state of tension that he would soon head straight for an ulcer, Clarice and Jasper immediately contacted him and told him what Mike had said.

Rich, who had been almost due for a classical attack of anxiety neurosis, suddenly did a right-about-face and began to appreciate the problems he was creating for his own body. Once he had brought his system back into proper alignment, his half-formed ulcer began to heal, and he eventually became a much calmer and more philosophical individual.

Another of Clarice's brothers, Jim, had achieved a position of authority in the world of journalism; but dealing with the foibles of local society had bred in him a disenchantment with humanity as a whole.

Mike counselled Clarice thus: "Mum, I want you to tell him that this bitterness could end up in a serious operation for gall-stones. If you can persuade him to take a refresher course in the humanities, he will soon get back in trim. Let him re-learn some of the basic truths, and his aggressions will go off the boil."

When he was told this, Jim adopted his usual defensive tactics; but his wife Joan confided to Clarice that he had had trouble with his gall-bladder for years, and she felt that Mike's advice was accurate and urgent.

Jasper realised that Jim must now face up to the havoc his tough exterior had created for him before his health broke down under the dead weight. He knew he would do no personal soul-searching until after the sky had fallen; it was vital that he overcome his store-bought cynicism, not only for his own sake but for the sake of his whole family.

The next time the two brothers-in-law were skirting gingerly round the edge of the problem, a golden shaft of light suddenly penetrated Jasper's mind, disclosing the deep, inarticulate love that lay in Jim's heart for his fellow man; a heart so compassionate that the suffering it caused him was well-nigh unbearable. Never again did Jasper tease him to test his defenses: instead he became over-involved, as if the fault lay with himself, and that he must personally restore Jim to a state of grace. So much so that Mike soon jocularly advised him: "I can see you in the pulpit of a Church yet, haranguing a captive congregation! Blimey, Jasper; maybe you ought to become a revivalist, so you can put a *real* fear of death into your gullible flock!"

Jasper collapsed with a yell of laughter, for nothing so hypocritical could have been further from his mind, and the matter seemed to end, for the time being. But after they had thoroughly discussed Jim's problem, Mike returned to the earlier subject in a more serious vein. "Dad, pretty soon you will be asked to address a conventional church gathering," he began. "I want you to accept the offer; and I don't want you to prepare a text — I'll try to inspire you when the time is ripe. Do you have enough faith in me? You know the way I worked it with MacGregor? — I can do the same with you."

Jasper was far from enamoured by this unexpected turn of events. He protested that it would be much to embarrassing to appear before a large flock, only to be struck dumb at the psychological moment because he hadn't prepared anything to say! He was, after all, an orthodox lawyer with a responsible local practice.

"Okay, Dad," said Mike cheerfully. "If it'll make you any happier, I'll slap an icy cold hand on the back of your neck, just as you start to speak! But seriously, Dad, when you face the congregation, an elder brother will make his presence felt by hanging a golden cross round your neck. When you feel it press against your chest, you'll know that *we* are there in full force to inspire you." Jasper immediately wanted to know who the "we" comprised, and Mike answered: "Why, Heather and me, of course!"

Nothing more was said about the matter until about four weeks later, when a small, pleasant-faced woman came into Jasper's office, sat down opposite him, and announced: "Mr. Swain, you have *got* to help us! We invited a guest speaker to address our congregation on Sunday. Yesterday he collapsed, and today he is in hospital with a coronary. So we want you to address our congregation instead!"

Jasper, thoroughly disconcerted, immediately answered: "Not me! I am *far* too corrupted by the world to be a parson! You've come to the wrong man!"

"No, I haven't," this lady insisted. "You're the one who's going to come and address us!"

Jasper then explained that he couldn't oblige them, that particular weekend, because he would be in Johannesburg.

But the now familiar shaft of golden light lit up his mind, and Mike's voice echoed in his ears: "Promise you will go, Dad!"

Jasper had the decency to forego further alibis and pretended to consult his diary. Then, albeit still reluctantly, he agreed to oblige the good lady.

When she asked him what subject he would prefer to speak on, the shaft of light again penetrated his mind and the words *Survival after Death* came echoing into his head.

Calmly he said: "Survival after death." The little old lady expressed her approval and made her departure, and Jasper proceeded to give a very good imitation of a man mentally kicking himself round the room.

Although his work called for him to give voice in the law courts every day of his life, Jasper felt that a bewigged judge in a court, and a large congregation in a church, were fish of entirely contrasting species! Nevertheless, he went home and announced to Clarice and Kevin that he had agreed to address a church congregation. With immodest glee and delight, Clarice and Kevin expressed every intention of accompanying him.

To Jasper's further chagrin, the local press the next day announced his debut officially.

The die was cast, the Rubicon would have to be crossed!

Jasper felt that he had been let in for the humiliation of his life, and there was no escape; so he contented himself with leaning heavily on Mike's assurance that no preparation would be necessary. Every now and again, however, his mind drifted to the subject of this talk, and he would imagine himself standing in the pulpit, looking into the eyes of a vast congregation, and not knowing what to say!

When the Swain family duly arrived at the church, it was already fairly full. Eventually the time came when Jasper had to enter the pulpit and deliver the address.

As he took his place there, he suddenly felt an icy hand on the nape of his neck, and the whole of his body shivered to the chill of its touch.

Jasper found himself instinctively thinking: "Oh, thank God! That shows Mike's around! I'm not going to be ditched at the last minute!" He stood looking down at the congregation, and a terrible pressure made itself felt on his chest. He thought: "Ha, this is the cross Mike told me about!"

For the next hour, to his own utter surprise, Jasper talked fluently about death and the transfer of the soul to the world of spirit. He could remember talking, he was aware of the rapt attention in the church, and inside him there welled up an enveloping desire to console these people; to convince them that there was indeed no death; therefore no reason to fear this perfectly natural translation, this re-birth, into the infinite world of light.

When he finished, he retired to the vestry; from there he re-entered the church from the back and sat next to Clarice and Kevin. He was rewarded by the profound approval he saw in the eyes of his wife and son. Now, at long last, he felt that he had contributed something, no matter how small, to the help of his fellow man.

Jasper now comprehended the way public speakers grip the minds of their audiences. It sobered him up: and it made a much wiser and more understanding man of him. Nor could he help but smile when he thought that, out of the glancing ray of light which he hoped had struck home to the hearts of his hearers, he himself had received the greater, the more wonderful illumination.

A member of the congregation that night was a young lady of twenty called Dene, who had been engaged to a pilot. The day Mike and Heather were cremated had been the day that Dene was to have been married; but a month earlier her fiancé had been flying a group of businessmen to a development scheme in northern Natal. While they were flying low over the rise of its hills, as instructed by the engineers, a high tension power line suddenly loomed in front of the plane. This line having only been erected a few months before, had not been marked on the aerial maps. The plane exploded with a blinding flash, and the pilot's body was found many hours later in a nearby gully.

MacGregor had known Dene and her fiancé extremely well; it was he who had been asked to perform their marriage ceremony. He was now called upon to assist Dene in her terrible hour of trial.

Dene refused to accept the death of her fiancé. He had been a vibrant, vital man, bubbling over with healthy exuberance. He

45

had been snatched away from her in such tragic circumstances that she had retired into a pall of silent indifference until she heard of the death of Mike and Heather. Then her heart had gone out to the bereaved parents she had never met, and by giving love and sympathy to them, life began to return to her own heart. Then she heard Jasper was to address the church, and she realised the subject, Survival after Death, was one he especially would understand.

When she listened to him that Sunday, she knew at once that he was not talking from theory. Nor was he bible-thumping; but merely told them what had happened to *him*, and told it in simple honesty. She listened wraptly, slowly began to understand and, for the first time, to accept what Jasper had accepted; the sure knowledge that her young lover still existed, the knowledge that there is no death. Slowly an enormous load lifted from her. Jasper later learned from her family that from that night onward, Dene began the road back to a normal existence.

He was deeply grateful to hear this, for he felt that even if she had been the only convert in the congregation, Mike's effort would certainly not have been in vain.

He was approached for weeks afterwards by church members who wanted to know more about the existence of the world of soul.

Jasper, making no claim to be an expert in such matters, would merely tell them what he himself had undergone. But this was proof enough that death is but a re-birth *for he had lost his fear of dying.*

Next time he talked to Mike, his son was jubilant. They had achieved far more than either had hoped — the head of his brotherhood had been overjoyed when the results proved to be greater than the elders had anticipated.

Mike said it was now time to raise the issue of MacGregor again. He urged Jasper to invite him to dinner. "He has come to an impasse in his relations with the Church," he explained "You'll have to sit him down and bang some sense into his head! And, Dad; don't lose your cool if you hear me prompt you from the wings!"

Jasper, confident now that he could now rank as a redoubtable mouthpiece for his son, promised not to 'lose his cool'.

Mike had always hero-worshipped MacGregor; now he could repay his old mentor 'in person', as it were, for the moral strength and courage he had given to the two bereaved families. Apart from this, Clarice and Jasper themselves had always wanted to reward MacGregor for having been such a staunch friend, so Jasper made a few discreet inquiries and learned that MacGregor had never been able to afford a really impressive fountain pen. A gold-plated Waterman was purchased forthwith, to be presented to him when he came to dinner.

MacGregor, full of his usual good cheer, was duly presented with the fountain pen. His face was a study of blank surprise, then embarrassment, then touchingly heartfelt pleasure. He had never sought any fee for his services; he had even refused to accept payment from the undertaker; but he was overcome by the sentiments underlying the gift of the pen; the appreciation of his work as a pastor, and Jasper and Clarice's profound love for him as a man.

It was soon clear that Mike's words were only too true. They knew nothing of MacGregor's personal battles and doubts, nor that his heart had been left with a girl in the Old Country; but after they had sounded him out, MacGregor confessed that he was on leave of absence from the Church until he found out, in his own heart and soul, whether he could ever become a worthy shepherd of His sheep. Only God alone knew the agony it had caused him to make this decision.

He had discussed the matter with the Bishop, who had advised him that all those who undertook the spiritual welfare of their fellow men went through the same battle; so, rather than accept MacGregor's resignation, he had advised an indefinite leave of absence instead.

When dinner was over, Clarice quietly disappeared, leaving MacGregor and Jasper facing one another in the sitting room.

Taking Jasper by surprise, MacGregor at once said quietly: "Jasper, you have a message for me from Mike, haven't you?"

"What gave you that idea?" parried Jasper.

"I've been a little psychic ever since I was a kid," said MacGregor, "so get cracking old man!"

Mike had not given him any forewarning of the conflict going on in MacGregor's life, so Jasper sat back and thought to himself: "Well, Mike? You'd better begin prompting me tout suite!"

Almost at once, the clear golden shaft lit up his mind, showing him a picture of the war in MacGregor's heart.

No longer in doubt, he said to MacGregor: "Which is your toughest problem?" and straightaway answered the question himself out of the top of his head.

When he had finished speaking, MacGregor looked at him for a long time, and then said: "*You* see, as nobody else has ever seen, this struggle going on within me. It is obvious that only Mike could have told you.

"I have never felt I was good enough to be a minister. I still can't believe that I actually became one! In England, before ordination, the conductor of the retreat told me the Church would have to wait a long time if she only accepted perfect servants. He said that I was the 'copybook ordinand', wanting to call it quits before the first shot had been fired!"

He chatted freely now, and the two men could have spent the balance of the night thrashing out the pros and cons, for MacGregor the inscrutable was at last baring his soul to another human being. Jasper was staggered as he listened to the complexity of the problems facing his guest, but together they tackled them all from every conceivable angle.

Then, once again, came this sudden shaft of golden light; and in his mind's eye, Jasper saw the true nature of the conflict between MacGregor and his Church. Mike showed him that MacGregor was confusing *two* battles; a personal one with himself, and another with the Church. He pointed out what MacGregor had forgotten: that he served a merciful Master. Human frailties notwithstanding, he must occupy himself solely with the Work itself.

"I know one thing," announced MacGregor firmly. "The Devil wouldn't tell a body to get on with a job for God! I shall go to the Bishop and withdraw my resignation!"

"Well, Dad," said Mike, "seeing that you will eventually join me here on this side of the Great Divide, let's talk about the process of death from *your* point of view first. There are three ways of moving into our world from yours. The first is to come as I did, with the violence of an abrupt end. The second is to come as a result of the body breaking down; for example, from illness or old age. *The third way, the logical way, is to come to us with full and conscious understanding of why it is happening.*

48

"Now I know that the third way rang a bell in your mind, so let's discuss it here and now.

"For a start, the soul that inhabits your body operates like a system of electrical impulses. Most people call it the etheric body. The New Testament agrees that human personality *does* survive the barrier of death. The Master Jesus Himself revealed His etheric body to His disciples. He even showed them the nail holes in His hands, remember? In other words, He *recreated* His earthly body out of etheric matter; out of the electric impulses which had activated the flesh-and-blood body. Being a Master, He was enlightened enough to do so, for a Master has full control of all the energy levels on the earth and can bend them all to His will.

"I often marvel at His humility when He was hanging on the cross; allowing Himself to be *thrown* from that life into this one, when all the might of Heaven was at His command! By the flick of a finger, He could have unleashed powers unknown to man! Yet He let them do to Him what they would, even though they subjected His physical body to unspeakable torture. When I think of the example of the Master, I regret I did not study His teachings a bit more intelligently when I was on earth. It's only when you arrive here that you realise how His teachings have been twisted to suit the end of men; including His attitude to the process of dying. When the Bible says: 'the silver cord is severed and the golden bowl is broken', it uses precise and clear-cut language. When you're asleep, your soul can travel to these planes where I exist; but it maintains contact with your mortal body by a thin luminous thread which the Bible calls the Silver Cord. This anchors the soul to the body until the need for sleep has been satisfied.

"Sometimes a recollection of the soul's journey filters down this silver cord to the mind of the sleeper in the form of a very vivid dream. But the human mind is fallible, having been conditioned since childhood to certain water-tight beliefs, and so the message transmitted by the silver cord can become garbled and incoherent. Sometimes, when the soul observes its own body on the earth doing something contrary to Divine Will, the physical conscience it lashes into such ferocious nightmares that the poor sleeper is terrified into recalling the soul to his body. An awakening in a cold sweat of terror follows.

"When death comes, the process is exactly the same, except that when the soul detaches itself from the body, the silver cord is severed completely. That is the beginning and the end of the mechanics of death.

"There are of course a few minor conditions involved. Firstly, no soul can ever pass over into these worlds *unless it has given its consent;* and here I don't mean a conscious consent, because the conscious mind is only a minor extension of the soul. The conscious mind may assume that death is approaching, but it is the soul itself that must give its consent before the process can take place.

"Imagine, Dad, that you are an old man with reasonable faith in your Creator. You have been a fairly good Christian all your life, trying to live the laws as they were laid down by the Master, Jesus. Admittedly you broke them when the temptation became too great, but you feel in your own mind that the Great One will forgive your run-of-the-mill transgressions.

"That would be your first mistake. There is no judging, when you pass over into our world. As I said before, your soul vibrates at a certain rate; and when it passes over, it will vibrate at a similar rate here.

"If you have lived a deceitful life on earth, your soul vibrations will be very sluggish; you will go to a low plane here, on which your fellows will be similar to you in mind and deed. You can imagine the in-fighting which goes on among such people! You meet the application of the law: 'As ye sow, so shall ye reap'.

"But the actual act of dying is as simple as dozing off after lunch. A drowsy feeling fills the whole of your body with relaxing comfort. You can still see, with your earthly eyes, the room about you. Then you notice that there are all kinds of new people standing around your bed; people that you once knew; such as parents, a favourite uncle, a friend who passed over many years sooner: the joy of seeing them again takes your mind off everything else. They take you by the hand and lift you to your feet. This invariably causes you to look back at the bed, and to your surprise you or your mortal shell, is still lying there. You say aloud: 'But how can I be here with you people, and yet still be lying there on the bed?' Only then do you realise that this is death.

"So now you are taken by your friends to the world where you now belong. As you move out of the room together, you pass through what appears to be a fog or mist. It is not dense, you can see for about six feet ahead of you; and because you know and love the people you are with, you follow them gladly. This mist is caused by the dispersing of your etheric body, which has served as the guardian of your material body. The etheric body, now that death has intervened, leaves the material body and seeks to attach itself to the soul. But as you move up towards the rarer planes, the etheric matter cannot follow; so it forms the mist which obscures your vision for a few seconds. When you step out of the mist, the etheric matter returns to the universal reservoirs.

" 'The silver cord and the golden bowl' are merely symbolic words, signifying the end of the earth experience. Nature wraps you in a blanket of sleep; a person, even if he is terrified of dying, merely falls asleep. In his sleep, he dreams that he is still in the same room; but actually he is passing to our Golden World.

"*Believe me, Dad, it is ten times more dangerous and unpleasant to be born into your world, than it is to leave it!* Being born is a painful, risky process; and none of us contemplate it with any degree of pleasure. And yet all you people on the earth fear death. I feared it when I was there; the few times I *did* think of it, which were very, very few!

"Now let us deal with the conscious passing over of someone who is familiar with the process of death. There are very few such people in the western world today, for they are mostly advanced souls who only returned to your earth to perform a specific task; to bring about an advance in thought, or encourage a particular philosophy. When the time comes for them to return to their proper realm, they do so, believe me, with the utmost relief and joy! They tidy up their earthly affairs, then unhurriedly ask the blessings of the Great One. Then they simply lift out of their bodies and come straight to the plane where they belong. Nothing could be simpler or more benign.

"The third means of passing over is as I did. Remember Dad; although my *conscious* mind didn't know I was about to return here, my soul did. Three days before the accident, I knew somehow, subconsciously that my earth life was coming to a close. My actual passing, I have already described to you. Both Heather and I were lifted out of our bodies *before* the collision. There was no pain, no shock. This process is the same in all and every form of violent death. If it appears violent from your end; believe me, it is *only* from your end; never from ours!

"In the case of the rather backward soul; we place him into a deep torpor as soon as we take charge. When he arrives in this world, he wakes in what appears to him to be a hospital ward. The realisation filters to him that he is safe and being well looked after; then it gradually dawns on him that there are no doctors or nurses in this hospital; no bandages and no surgical instruments. He himself feels no pain; so his next move is to get out of bed and start exploring, to find out what sort of hospital this is. Only then does he realise that he has successfully passed over. It is wonderful to watch his amazement and relief when he realises he is more alive than ever.

"It takes some time, quite some time, for all this to register completely; often his first reaction is to go back to bed for another couple of days to get used to the idea of what has happened to him!

"Then one of the elders visits him and answers all the unasked questions in his mind. You see, the laws of creation are not as easily grasped by these backward souls as they are by their more experienced brothers.

"By the same token, if there is not enough love in the heart of a new arrival here, his ability to adapt to a world that operates on love is likewise backward. Which is a good thing; because the first thing he would do would be to create weapons, and then use them to establish power over his fellow souls!

"Not that they can hurt one another; their new bodies are indestructable; so when they finally realise the futility of picking up a club and bopping a neighbour over the head with it, they feel very hard done by. But they end up realising that they'll only win by living in peace with their fellows. Gradually, (and you can watch the idea take hold), unselfish gestures emerge, and finally the texture of the soul purifies itself enough to enable them to reach a clearer, more harmonious plane; and as things become clearer still, so do they advance to even more resolved planes.

52

"There is one very foolish method of coming here. By suicide. This is a futile action for all concerned. When someone on the earth plane feels so restricted, so cramped, so frightened, that he sees no solution to it — when in fact, he can no longer face up to the day-to-day burdens that confront everyone else in your world — he thinks that committing suicide will be an easy way out and will punish his 'tormentors' at the same time.

"When his soul comes here, it is immediately placed in a state of rest . . . until the jangling dislocations of the suicide have subsided. Then he is immediately sent back to earth to inhabit a new body. Once again he finds himself a mortal man; *but he retains no recollection of his previous history.*

"What is more, in this second life of his, he is going to be confronted by exactly the same problems. If he fails a second time, the same process will occur and continue to occur until he learns to face his problems rather than escape them.

"Throughout, he will be surrounded by the love of the Great One and guarded by his brothers; but he must solve his problem without any aid from anyone. Once he has faced it and solved it, there is no further danger of him committing suicide. At the same time he is developing the strength of mind that he will need when *he* eventually learns to be a Creator, as his Great Father was before him.

"So, if you want a frustrating round-trip ticket up to our world and right back down to yours again, Dad, commit suicide! It will get you nowhere fast!

"Originally, when our souls first took on the forms of men, we were still sons of God: with His divine sanction we chose for ourselves how we wanted to look, and how we would develop. All divine law is predicated on this freedom of choice. *We* decide, Dad. We ourselves decide what we are going to do. If it conflicts with any of the Divine rules, then *we* have to correct our error. Remember the miser and the drunkard, when they came over here? They punished themselves very, very effectively! Yet no one sat in judgement on them. No one decreed any punishment or penalty. That is because — and I reiterate it — these worlds are created of love, Dad; the infinite love of the Great One. As we pray to Him, a blue shaft of light goes up to the heavens — then it turns to gold; and His infinite peace flows down it to surround us.

"When 'men of the cloth' get up here; oh, Dad, it is terrible to watch their self-recrimination and their soul-searching when they realise what they taught on earth was too often wide of the mark; even though they merely taught what they themselves had been taught. They need all our help and comfort as they battle against terrifying images of devils and hell fire . . . which, in truth, do not exist here or anywhere else!

"But there are, on the lower planes, souls who need the security of a church, and the advice of a minister, before their faith can take articulate form. They attend beautiful cathedrals and they listen avidly to all the sermons. But the only ritual they *hear*, here, is the true litany!

"When Heather last talked to you, she told you about the kitten that adopted her when she came here. Now she has a dog. There is every kind of tame animal and bird in these realms . . . proof once again of the law of love! When you create a bond with an animal on earth plane, that bond is powerful enough to bring him here when he dies. He is cared for until his master passes over to our plane. When animals arrive here, it is wonderful to see them gambolling with one another . . . lions and tigers alongside tabby cats . . . why, some Burmese mahouts even bring their elephants with them! All of them survive the journey because of the love and care showered on them by everybody here.

"We hear birds singing wherever we go. If I happen to admire their song, they immediately respond to my thought; they will perch on my finger and show off their colours and their musical range! We never cease to marvel at the infinite variety of happiness on these planes, Dad.

"When I first arrived here, I felt no sudden jar at my passing. As I told you, we were lifted in the air and I took Heather's hand, and together we saw the cars collide. Then Uncle Mark was suddenly standing beside us. He explained that we had been through such a terrible collision that we were no longer in the land of the living. I was too surprised to ask him how he knew, although I *did* have a hunch I was dead, and it seemed perfectly natural that he had come to take charge of us.

"I decided that Heather and I couldn't do better than go along with him; so we did. It was simply a question of ascending gradually into the sky, until all of a sudden we were in this beautiful pasture. I can't say exactly how long it took us to leave the earth plane. It was rather much like flipping a radio dial from one station to another. When you turn the knob, you take for granted that another station will be awaiting your pleasure; you don't think there's anything *unusual* about it. That was how we moved from your world to our new one. All our family, even the ones we didn't know when we were on the earth, were here to welcome us. They made us feel wanted, and very much at home!

"That's why I took so long to realise that the news of our death would not be accepted by you as it was on this plane. It was only then, Dad, that I could actually feel the terrible pull of the grief that you and Mum were suffering. You remember when you wanted to punish the driver of the other car? When I felt that terrible resolve hardening itself in your heart, I knew I had to return and make myself known to you. Nothing else would have altered your stubborn determination to revenge our deaths.

"Before you could raise yourself up to *this* plane, you would have to raise your vibrations to the speed of mine. Likewise, when I need to regress myself back to *your* world, I have to reduce my vibrations to their slowest rate. This isn't easy, Dad: some of it is downright painful. It's like putting on a strait-jacket. I have to constrict myself more and more, like the Rabbit in *Alice in Wonderland*, until my vibrations are moving as slowly as yours.

"Not that I'm trying to blow my own trumpet, you understand, but I *am* one of the few here who have been able to manage it. I can move from my world to yours by my own free will. Heather can do it too, now. But I would say that ninety-five per cent of the souls at this level are completely unable to manifest at the earth level. Maybe in moments of urgency, they can appear momentarily to their loved ones on earth, but they wouldn't promise to guarantee it.

"Perhaps the most important message we can send you from here — if you can get it across for me — is that grieving, weeping, and wishing for the soul of the departed to return, are the worst things that you people can do to someone who has just died.

"You see, wherever there is a bond of love, there is an unbroken line of communication.

"When you grieve for someone you love, your sorrow is immediately transmitted to him in his new world — a most beautiful world — but he cannot come back to the earth plane to comfort his mourners. He hasn't had time to master the art of slowing down his vibrations until you can see him or hear him. This puts him in a hell of a quandary — he is torn between a desire to comfort his loved ones, *knowing it to be impossible*, and a need to adjust himself to his bright new surroundings.

"So please, Dad, tell those who are still on earth not to grieve for those of us who have come over here. I know it's impossible to ask them to rejoice; yet we on *this* side rejoice when the soul of an old friend comes here. I would ask the bereaved to sit and think of their loved ones instead of themselves. They will soon forget their own sorrows. Tell them, please, just to send their love and kindly thoughts for a calm journey and a happy arrival, for the friend they have lost is already secure in this world of warmth and happiness.

"Send wave upon wave of love. This will help the newly dead to stabilise, because it convinces them of the validity of both spheres of existence. This is perhaps the most important thing I want you to put into this book.

"When I first explored this new world, I felt I was coming back to a familiar landscape I already knew well. After one good look around, I soon satisfied myself that everything was in good order in my Father's house!

"Because I can keep in contact with your plane, I know how your young people think and feel; and Heather and I are often able to give them a helping hand. Because we both want to get busy and *do* something, the elders have told us that we are of the most use when we help the young who are about to arrive here by way of violence.

"One of the elders always tells us by telepathy *who* to help, and *when*. This is usually ten to fifteen minutes before the final moment occurs; then we have enough notice to meet the soul and escort him to wherever he is meant to go. He may not know that we are with him, but the Great One gives us the power to comfort and console, which we then transmit to the soul we are protecting.

"When we are given a case where two cars are about to collide, for example, we lower our vibrations until that soul can actually see us: thus his attention is diverted from the violence about to engulf him. Once we are sure that nothing more can be done to avert his death, we take him by his hands and lift him out of his earthly body.

"When they are evolved souls — and, evolved souls are peculiarly inquisitive! — they are fascinated by who we are and what we are doing: it is only much later that we show them the violence that had been done to their earthly shells. Believe me, Dad, they are more than willing to accept the fact that they are dead! And as we lift them up to *our* level, we equalise our own vibrations to *their* vibrations as they change from coarse to fine. After that, their own loved ones appear, and our share of that particular job is done.

"Do you recall the young high school boy who was killed in Durban in circumstances similar to mine? Dad, we were there: it was us who helped him over. He and I had known each other casually while we were both alive, so he was relieved and, believe you me, delighted to see me! He knew that I had already passed over, but it still took him a while to realise the significance of it, when I showed him the mess made by the two cars after they had collided!

"Heather and I have specialised in this kind of 'first aid' for about four months of your earth time; and though I'm not an expert on the subject, I'm beginning to suspect that there are discrepancies between our time and yours.

"Whenever you ask me to estimate *our* time, I always have to multiply everything by seven to bring it up to the speed of *your* time. For example, when something is about to happen in our world, I can see it about a month before it happens; but in earth-time, it would happen seven months from now! If this sounds complicated, look at it from a financial point of view — you would get seven days pay to my one!

"More and more, Heather and I are being called on to help teenagers who pass over under the most negative circumstances. *I am referring to the 'Russian Roulette' kids who get hooked on drugs.*

"Too many adolescent deaths occur as a result of drugs; some because of the rank poison in the drug itself, and others because their normal instinct for self-preservation had been blotted out by their senseless addiction to narcotics. These kids abruptly terminate their life-spans because they could find no other logical way out of the snarl-ups. Drugs can cause fatal malfunctions of the brain at many different levels of consciousness.

"Our elders are satisfied that Heather and I know how to bring these toxic minds here with a minimum of 'spoilage', but we both felt we could do a more thorough job if we had our own private headquarters, so we persuaded one of the elders to approve a small cottage hospital where these shattered youngsters can adapt themselves to the new environment.

"Reality never imprints itself on the memory of a drug addict, because the mind had ceased to function normally. Therefore these kids have no idea how they got here, when they wake up in our world. They not only have no memory of the drug they have taken; they cannot recall what happened to them while they were under its influence.

"Therefore our first job is to reconstruct the damaged memory so they can recall how they felt while they were still 'high' on that particular type of drug. Having re-created its effect in their minds, we then re-create the memory of their passing.

"Then we gradually lighten their sleep until they can remember 'a dream' in which they died. Not until they have fully regained consciousness do they realise that the dream was not a dream, but their actual passing over.

"Once they have accepted that, there is nothing to stop them joining their families and taking their rightful place on these golden planes.

"We are particularly careful to ensure that there are no negative after-effects; no guilt. We *never* allow pain or suffering to accompany the passing over of the soul.

"Although I have already said this, I feel I should repeat that it is far less painful for a mortal to die than to be born. Lest even a trace of fear linger in the mind of one of these young drug addicts as he passes over, he is placed into such a deep sleep that the transition takes place without his knowledge. He will only learn what has happened after he regains consciousness in this world of love.

58

"Another of our duties is to take these newly translated souls with us on our rounds of the various halls of learning. Invariably they meet with us afterwards to tell me what they have listened to. As there is no night or day here, these can be long sessions; but it is immensely rewarding to watch this new knowledge exciting the imaginations of our new arrivals.

"At the moment, seven of them always join us on our rounds. Whenever one of them has a problem we cannot solve, I contact the nearest elder telepathically. Either he appears and solves the problem for us, or he sends one of the senior-ranking souls: there is never any false pride here about giving and taking advice.

"In your world, an inquisitive child who eternally asks questions very soon gets the brush-off. His questions are nearly always ignored, whether they reflect intelligence or idle curiosity. Up here, curiosity is a highly prized commodity, because the more curious you are, the more knowledge you stand to absorb. All the wisdom of the ages is available here, so a healthy curiosity can keep you gainfully employed for a very long time!

"We are particularly favoured in this sphere because the *akashic records* are available to us. Your every thought, deed and action while you are on your earth is permanently recorded on the rarified vibrations of our etheric world. These records can never be obliterated. Whenever one of the Great Masters needs to measure the development of a particular soul, he merely tunes into that particular wave-length, and the akashic records will reveal his innermost thoughts. It is like watching a three-dimensional colour T.V. You see everything exactly as it happened, as though you were there in the flesh.

"I hadn't been here long before I wished I had studied the Master Jesus more closely while I was still on earth; and right there and then I was allowed to view his life in the akashic records exactly as he lived it. I was so very deeply moved that one of the leaders said to me: 'Now, my son, look at it from the point of view of the world he inhabited. Here was a man who left home at a very early age and involved himself in a kind of radical thinking; he travelled from state to state preaching a doctrine which was considered as extreme as communism is today. He was against interference with an individual's right to complete freedom. You can imagine how welcome those ideas were, when the Great One was alive! He was chased out of most towns just one jump ahead of the local police!

" 'Eventually he returned to his home town. There he collided with the Roman authorities, who promptly executed him. Look at that from a non-partisan point of view. What a waste of human endeavour!'

"Dad, I thought about that for a long time before I realised just how different the same set of facts can look, depending on the eye of the observer! The life of the Master was the most perfect lived on earth. He taught profounder truths than any of the other Great Ones who returned to your world. Do beg, borrow or steal a copy of the *Aquarian Gospel*. Although it was first published in 1926, it is couched in simple colloquial language. We hope that it will come into its own in the 1970s in your world, for it is an uncorrupted text. Besides which, the highly evolved spirits in charge of your earth's ultimate destiny are very much aware that the Great Master is preparing to return as He promised.

"I believe it is His presence, as He prepares to lower his vibrations, that is creating the disturbance at your mortal level. As He slows his vibrations, the closer He draws to your world; and likewise His power agitates your make-shift values.

"Another thing I now understand better is the problem of nervous breakdowns. I used to think that bad nerves were the exclusive property of people whose minds swung aimlessly from one obsession to another. Now I realise that when a man on the earth-plane starts to become more mature, he comes into conflict with most of the attitudes he had previously formed; particularly when they were wrong! As life is not going to change, *he* must. You can imagine the upheaval in his habit-patterns, when he can no longer trust any part of his previous attitude to the world around him!

"We up here have a very real compassion for a mortal who undergoes a nervous breakdown, because we realise it is the birth-pangs of his determination to grow more mature. He is beginning to understand how the laws of God control the world about him, and this leads him to cast a critical eye at his fellow men, as he begins to wonder what makes them tick. When he does that, he is beginning the long upward journey to reconciliation with his spiritual Father.

"By the same token, I feel that most of the misfits in society — the tramps, the drunkards and the drug addicts — are undergoing a drastic purification of their minds and souls. They can no longer conform to the norm, because they have begun to suspect that there is something more vital to life than its facade. So don't be too quick to dismiss the contribution of the down-and-out drunk. More likely than not, he is undergoing a very essential spring-cleaning. Once he is over it, he will make a far better contribution to his community than he was ever able to before.

"Man is always trying to assimilate; but the moment he does not pay lip service to society's bogus ideas of outward decorum, it bars its doors to him. When his kind come here, Dad, they are made doubly welcome. We also find that when an atheist arrives at these doors, having died denying the existence of God, *he had actually admitted the existence of God, in order to be able to deny Him!* So that brother, too, has started on the steep homeward path of return to his eternal Father."

The fact that Mike had said that his special task was the care of his own generation renewed Jasper's curiosity. Why had Mike's particular generation developed such an obsession for lethal drugs? Why did they have to blot out the normal world? Why weren't they prepared to accept it as it existed around them? Or *was* this world so desirable after all?

"No, it's not!" answered Mike's voice. "Every fish that swims in the sea adjusts its life to the patterns made by the tides, the rocks and the muddy water from the rivers. It knows that these conditions are an everlasting reality to which it must conform to survive. Every bird flying in the air accepts the wind, the clouds, the lightning and thunder, as being hazards which exist, and therefore govern his world of existence. You as a man, Dad, think you have to bide by the laws of morality which exist in your world; but I have to tell you now that a lot of the values you believe to be essential are no such thing! They are obsolete relics from your formative years, when you were promptly whacked if you disagreed with your school teacher. Respect for your elders simply meant that they could subject you to their own rules and regulations, whether the logic escaped you or not! You *had* to conform to them, but it was a submission based on intimidation instead of reason.

"Up here, before we respect a rule, we familiarise ourselves with the *necessity* for respecting it. There is no coersion involved; it is simply a question of arriving at a sensible conclusion. If you don't want to obey it, you needn't; but in that case, you accept the consequences.

"I always have a great deal to discuss with the young souls, after their transition to this plane. I often have to ease them out of the beliefs that were bashed into them while they were still on your world, usually by the members of your generation. I omit you and Clarice from that generalisation, because you allowed me to make most of my own decisions myself; but too many youngsters in your world are forced to attend Sunday school at gunpoint in order to learn what Christianity is all about; and when they are finally confirmed in the Christian Church, they aren't allowed to question those beliefs in any manner, shape, or form — unless they want to suffer the disapproval of society in general.

"People no longer risk going to jail for being agnostics or followers of crack-pot religious cults; but this has only come about since the Second World War. And they're still regarded as lunatics!

"Don't mistake me. I'm not advocating the rejection of the established Church. Quite the opposite; I want you to begin to understand what Christianity is! I want you to go back and trace the origin of the Bible, and find out just how many of the real sermons of Jesus of Nazareth it actually contains.

"Peewits by the score have made so bold as to say that the Bible must be taken literally. If the words had come direct from Jesus himself, no one could take the slightest exception. But when you study the dogma of the Church, you will find it excommunicates any of its sheep who will not swallow the tampered texts, hook, line and sinker. You must accept without question that Christ, his Father, and the Holy Ghost, are an indivisible trinity, which they are not. Jesus was a simple, loving flesh-and-blood man. He stood as a great friend of the poor. He was a great healer, he comforted those in sorrow and, above all, the whole of his preaching reflects his love of our Eternal Father. He foretold the happiness that awaits us on this plane where I now exist; and he told us how to live our lives on earth so that we could learn the lessons we were sent there to learn. When you follow his teachings, how much easier your life becomes! But he was a reformer first and foremost, and he was made to suffer for his beliefs.

"The Church, however, says that he was crucified because he wanted to take the sins of humanity upon his own shoulders!

"Dad; can you, as a clear-thinking man, really believe that you can go out and cut your brother's throat, and because Jesus has already been crucified for your sin, it won't be taken into account when you are brought before your Maker? You have often used the expression: 'That is an escapist attitude bar none!'

"Jesus never claimed to be a scapegoat for the rest of humanity! He taught a simple religion of love and service to one's fellow man; and he advised us to 'honour our father and our mother'. Then why, in another portion of the same Bible, are we told that 'he who hates not his father and mother, and wife and children, yea, and his own life also, cannot be my disciple'? *That text was used as justification for the Inquisitions.*

"Jesus was a poor man who possessed nothing more than the clothes on his back. When you look at the ornate robes of the high church dignitaries, don't you wonder? Yet this same Church has set up national orphanages; it has set up a school system that educates the poor; it has led most of the humane movements in history.

"But the other side of the coin still remains. And the major issue in the minds of the young when they come here, is still this indigestible contrast between the simple parables of Jesus and the double-dutch rules-of-thumb of the established Church. This is why the young here condemn your generation for being two-faced: how else could you hope to practise the lessons taught by Jesus in one breath, and pay lip service to the business world, in the next?

"This is the biggest problem that I have to handle here. The young were born into your world with clean, clear eyes from these golden planes, and they found themselves in a world where the behaviour of their fellow men was hypocritical and craven. They came into your world seeking love, truth and brotherhood; instead they found fraud and oppression. Your double standard had thrown them into such confusion by the time they were sixteen, seventeen, eighteen years of age, that they felt they must either adapt themselves to it or try to escape, if only for an hour or two.

"As their bodies became more and more hardened to drugs, they increased the dosage to insure oblivion. And when that finally brings them here, Heather and I can only do the best we can."

Jasper, resigned to the fact that his own generation was 'square' and 'unreceptive', was most unhappy to find himself now cast in the role of deep-dyed villain.

The problem had to be tracked to its source, and in his determined effort to get to the truth, Jasper found that the first definitive breach between Christ and Church had come at the Council of Nicaea in AD 325, when Christianity became the new-fangled belief of the Roman Emperor Constantine.

The true instigator of this version of Christianity was the disciple Paul, who favoured the philosophy of the Stoics in the form adhered to by Philo. This version considered man to be two-fold: half of him was spirit and the other half was human, along with all its carnal appetites and earthly passions. Thus the body was a jail which imprisoned the spirit, which in turn eternally struggled to return to its heavenly origin.

Paul wholeheartedly subscribed to the logic of this doctrine; but whether Jesus believed it too is another matter, for he never came into personal contact with Paul. It was after he had been crucified that Jesus reproached him with: "Paul, Paul, why persecutest thou me?" It would be quite logical for Paul to have associated this sublime vision with his own pet theory. Furthermore, the other apostles seem to have been unimpressed by the letters of Paul. They preferred to let him go his own way. Never does Paul himself quote the teachings of Jesus *verbatim*. Coupled to this, the Gnostics held that God's plan of salvation would be brought to man through the personal intercession of the Son of God. Hence the crucifying of Jesus, coupled with Paul's own 'vision', made the Gnostic belief infallible to him — with one fallible difference: Paul considered that love was only a physical emotion and therefore dispensable.

It was the counter-Pauline school that believed that the

64

salvation of man would be achieved by the token-sacrifice of a symbolic redeemer; and this is the view still held by the established Church. How different contemporary faith might be, if it had abided by Paul's belief!

The earliest synoptic work, the *Gospel of St. Mark*, originated in AD 70. The *Gospel of St. Luke* appeared twenty years later in AD 90, and the *Gospel of St. Matthew* in AD 100. There is a fine distinction between these and the *Gospel of St. John*, which came into being in AD 110, for the *Encyclopaedia Brittanica* suggests that either the *Gospel of St. John* is inaccurate, or the synoptic gospels are. Added to this, Matthew and Luke appear to be copied from Mark, with independent alterations added: the enthusiasm of ancient writers for 're-interpreting' what they were copying was an accepted practice. Finally, most biblical experts now conclude that there is a missing manuscript, the *Quelle*, which fathered them all.

The early Church fathers conscientiously gathered up all the available literature, approved that which they felt to be 'inspired', and rejected the balance. The recent discovery of the *Gospel of St. Thomas* makes it obvious that John himself had dealt purely with the symbolic side of the teachings of Jesus. But the symbolic side of the teachings of Jesus is excluded from the Bible as we know it today.*

Constantine, when he wanted to re-establish the quasi-defunct Roman Empire, needed a unifying factor to inspire his people. His mother was already a Christian, so when he examined the teachings of Jesus of Nazareth, it was logical for him to feel that he had found his man.

He assembled the Council of Nicaea to formalise his new religion, but the arguments became so heated that confidential documents were flung over the council-chamber and many of the members came to bodily harm. When they finally compromised on a lame-duck solution, Constantine promptly overrode it and wrote his own version. This he forced them to sign on pain of excommunication.

---

* L. G. Rylands in *A Critical Analysis of the Four Pauline Epistles*: "Now that it has been demonstrated that Pauline Christianity was Gnostic, the connecting link is found. Pauline Christianity was evidently a development from the Pre-Christian Gnosticism."

Arius, the only council member who believed that Jesus was not only the Christ but an impeccable mortal inspired by God, was thereby defeated, and the Unitarian belief was thrown out of official Christianity along with its earliest champion.

When the Bishop of Alexandria now felt free to teach that God was unique and indivisible, Arius objected hotly; insisting that God, being divisible, had sent the spirit of Christ to inhabit the body of Jesus of Nazareth, *transforming him thereby into a Holy Soul in a mortal body.* This split the council wide open, and Constantine was once again more than happy to referee. Predictably, the Bishop of Alexandria won the day; and the misguided believers in the indivisibility of the Father, the Son, and the Holy Ghost, impressed their victory onto Christianity for evermore.

Eusebius had also found himself in the line of fire when Constantine ordered the council to sign the decree. Though he did so, he later confessed to his flock that 'the Creed is more creditable to the ingenuity of the Emperor than to his Candour!'

Jerome, in the year 384, candidly admitted that he had amended the early scriptures to bring them into line with what *he* thought had really happened. Our Holy Bible today is based on Jerome's Latin translation.

One of the worst body-blows to the Church was the appearance of the prophet Mohammed in the seventh century. When he conquered Palestine and Egypt, he was able to commandeer a third of God's children under his 'heathen' banner.

The idiocy of the unchristian Crusades, a direct result of the depredations of Mohammed, at least brought one merciful reform; the wounded were kept alive in hospitals instead of being spitted on the battlefields like carrion.

In 1054, Pope Leo IX decided to add the word 'filiogue' to the creed (meaning 'and from the son'). Because of this amendment, the Greek Orthodox Church broke away, and Leo promptly excommunicated everybody in it. From that day to this the Popes in the west and the Patres in the east have been at loggerheads.

With much-needed and long-overdue Reformation, the antic minds of the great men were set aglow again. Erasmus took a long, hard look at Christianity and felt the call to reform it, and

Luther and Calvin top-heavily followed suit. All of them were aware that the church militant of the Middle Ages had obliterated the humane creed of Jesus; but the sum total of their enthusiasm was simply the replacement of the old corruptions by freshly-minted synonyms.

And thus the voice of the Prince of Peace, even today, continues to languish obscured and unheeded.

Jasper had always held firm to the reasoning in Luke's Gospel, wherein Jesus made his own attitude perfectly clear by reading aloud from the Book of Isaiah: "The spirit of the Lord is upon me, because he has anointed me to preach His gospel to the poor. He has sent me to heal the broken-hearted, bring deliverance to the captive, and recovery of sight to the blind." Jesus then added to his listeners in the synagogue: "*This day is this scripture fulfilled in your ears.*"

Jasper, more and more unhappy as he came across so much that was contrary to these original concepts, put the problem to Mike, who turned to his elders for guidance.

The answer was wonderful in its clarity.

"Dad," said Mike, "when you look at *any* human being, you look at a son of God. And look what they get up to! They lie, they steal, they betray each other; they do everything that the Commandments forbid. Why is this the normal pattern? Because when their spirits were first demoted to material shape, our Father gave them the right to do whatever *they* felt they wanted to do. Some chose to do good, others to do ill. And it is *only* through these two channels that they learn and grow.

"When you have done ill, the law of *'as ye sow, so shall ye reap'* applies. So sit back and wait for ill to be done to *you*. And this law of cause-and-effect will continue to operate until it dawns on you that it is easier on you to obey the laws of the Great One. Otherwise you may have to continue making amends indefinitely!

"This is the process of purification wherein man, of his own free will, learns to act in harmony with Divine Law.

"And the Church is in *exactly* the same situation. It must go through the very purgatory it warns humanity to avoid, before it can practise what it preaches.

"So I don't really understand why you're getting into such a monumental flap. This is the right and proper form of evolution. This is your heritage as a son of God.

"It certainly won't help matters to turn your back on the Church. *On the contrary, re-involve yourself for all you're worth.* Put pressure on your ministers to abide by the original words of Jesus of Nazareth. After all, Dad, who has kept the teachings of Jesus alive for the last two thousand years? The same Church that keeps trying to crucify him all over again!

"The Church is man-made, Dad; it has all the defects that *you* have personally. So accept the Church for what it is; just as you accept yourself for what you are. Improve that which is wrong, and encourage that which is right; that way, you will eventually obtain perfection both for yourself and the Church you have learned to honour."

This indeed was the knock-out blow to Jasper's self-doubt.

It now occurred to Jasper that this process of being whacked over the head until one eventually followed the right path, must of necessity take more than one life. He had already lived half his present life without accepting the logic of this argument: all he had to show for it was the knowledge that he had done precious little more than take the wrong turning. So he expended the last of his 'question-and-answer period' to finding out whether Jesus had taught anything about reincarnation.

The earliest evidence for it lay in the works of the great Pythagoras, around 540 BC. He had claimed that he received the memory of all his previous incarnations as a gift from the god Mercury, along with a knowledge of what the soul experiences before birth and after death.

In 200 BC Plato himself had asserted: *"Soul is older than body. Souls are continuously born again into this life."*

This pagan credo of Plato, Aristotle, Numinius and Corrutus was compounded into a unified theme by one of the earliest church fathers. Origen, in AD 200: and the doctrine of re-birth came into being for the first time in the Christian faith.

In his book *Contracelsum*, Origen argues: 'Is it not more in conformity with reason that every soul is introduced into a body *according to its deserts and former actions?* Is it not rational that souls who have used their bodies to do the utmost possible good, would have a right to bodies with qualities superior to the bodies of others?'

But even after his death, Origen never wanted for enemies.

68

Early in the sixth century, under Theodora, the prostitute spouse of the Byzantine Emperor Justinian, a canonical council published the *Anathemas;* and teachings of Origen which until then had been revered by the selfsame council, were now thrown out of the Church. And if such a basic premise in the logic of God's purpose could be removed by a neurotic squabble in a secular hierarchy, how often has it been tampered with since then?

Certainly, 'as ye sow, so shall ye reap' grows very big teeth, viewed through the bright lens of the doctrine of reincarnation; and it makes uncommon good sense of the Master's parables, once one has the guts to put it into practice.

Jasper winced when he thought of how much he probably still had to repay; and yet surely, if he adhered to a positive interpretation of the credo, he could use the selfsame law to decrease his debit account?

"Argued like a true lawyer!" laughed Mike. "You're beginning to stand on your own two feet at last!"

"And how would *you* respond, if you were a lawyer?" Jasper parried.

"Suppose I must travel from 'Maritzburg to Durban as the main reason for my having incarnated this time. The means by which I get there *are strictly up to me;* whether I walk, cycle, fly, drive, or crawl on my knees pushing a sausage with my nose, the only rule is that I must try to get there in one piece. Do I *have* to reach Durban direct? Can I go via Isipingo? Can I bypass Durban altogether, and pin all my hopes on Isipingo? On which point of the compass do the lords of the horizon award their highest bonus? Only God knows; and He won't tell! The possibility that there may be other, better alternatives may continue to plague and pique me; but the law of Conservation of Energy, while a formidably powerful law, is elastic enough to allow me 100% for honest effort.

"Life is an obstacle race, and all one can see ahead is the heaving tarpaulin, as it engulfs a frailer brother who has panicked and lost his sense of direction. One can only press on regardless. If you try to sneak out sideways — or worse, retreat — the whole game is cancelled and you will have to start again from scratch.

"Believe in the simple function of love, as it lies rooted in the brotherhood of man and the Fatherhood of God. There you cannot go wrong. Crutches are all very fine when you have a broken leg; but once the leg is healed, they are merely vainglorious. *Always* remember that you are a son of God in your own right. You *must* look your Master in the face and claim your birthright.

"You alone are held responsible for your actions; so don't duck round corners hoping to evade the issue. *You* shape your life by the way you make your decisions: which explains why you excuse conduct in others that you would never excuse in yourself, because you know better!

"It's not an impossible task. In fact, it's a very simple one. Just let yourself bask in the golden light of eternal serenity, and go forth with love to meet your brothers in the universe. Your whole outlook will change. All you have to do is try it, '*till now, my father!*' We will meet again soon."

The significance of Mike's last words was lost on Jasper for the moment.

Thinking over Mike's argument concerning the true function of the Church, he now saw that religion, for so long administered by institutions, was actually something more personal. Every member of the Christian community had a right to select for himself the beliefs on which his life must depend for spiritual sustenance, for civilisation had reached the stage where it could no longer be spoon-fed by a benign computer. When he was a child, Jasper had been taught that the state existed solely for the benefit of the man-in-the-street: its function was to protect his rights and his property; but with the passing of time, it dawned on him that the individual exists for the state, not *vice versa*. Had this pattern repeated itself in religion?

Mike was highly delighted when Jasper brought the question to his attention. "Precisely!" he said. "It goes back as far as the legend that Jesus was not an ordinary man, born just as you and I were. Before the establishment could deify him in comfort, he had to become a figure of such exotic origin that no one would dare confuse him with an ordinary mortal.

"Because the natural origin of his birth has had to be concealed, you see the result in people like you and me, who were brought into the world by the common-or-garden process of evolution. We were told that we were too full of 'common clay' to be God-men! Another result was that sex became 'bad'. Therefore the clergy, as the mortal agents of the God-man, were forbidden to degrade their status by functioning as males of the species. They had to remain celibate."

Having listened to the hullabaloo concerning the celibacy of his local priests, Jasper knew why there would never be an official relaxation of this rule: it was based on the dubious legend of the virgin birth. Even Freud has conceded that every man must function in three main fields: work, play and sex. Denied such fundamental needs, anxiety neuroses could run rampant.

Similarly, the good of the institution had overriden the good of the individual on the issue of contraception. Jasper was only too familiar with the privations of those of his friends who wrestled with themselves to maintain a 'respectable' public image; and even more forsaken was the plight of the priest who was duty-bound to insist that his forbidding instructions were obeyed to the letter.

While Mike had never attempted to convert Jasper to a belief in Buddhism, he *had* offered an over-simplification of the Buddhist belief, in which God, having to spend twenty-four hours a day running His universes and galaxies, was happy enough when man himself got on with the business of improving his mind and soul. Ultimately, at the end of the uphill road, he is bound to come into contact with his Creator, even if, till then, He has been too busy to show a personal interest in each and every one of His children.

Jasper was able to appreciate this point of view, but his heart remained dedicated to the teachings of the man from Nazareth; for Mike had awakened in him a much more realistic belief in the teachings of Jesus.

One day, when nothing in the office seemed to be going right, Jasper's telephone rang and Mrs. Merrington's voice greeted him. "Come down here as quickly as you can!" she bade him. "I have something most important to tell you!" At that particular moment, Jasper felt too exhausted from a heavy day to drive a hundred-odd miles without a specific reason, but at almost the same moment he felt himself nudged by the shaft of golden light, and the word: "Go!" impressed itself on his mind, so he departed without further ado. He arrived at the end of the journey to be greeted by Mrs. Merrington's beaming smile. When he thought of the incessant hardships she had suffered, he was impressed anew by the inner strength and unshakable confidence she drew from her 'other voice'.

Her husband came in, and the three sat and chatted amiably until Nina Merrington bobbed her head at Jasper and said: "Have you any idea why I sent for you in such a hurry?"

"Not the slightest idea," Jasper assured her.

"Well, first," said Nina, "Mike wants you to know that he warned you in advance what is about to happen *would* happen!"

Then she went into a trance, and this time she used an entirely new method. She simply closed her eyes, and the next moment her features were irradiated by a golden light.

This light became stronger and stronger until Jasper felt that they must all be blinded by it. Then a shimmering translucence began to conceal her features, and all of a sudden Jasper found himself looking straight into Mike's eyes.

He glanced at Mr. Merrington and saw that he too was gazing with fixed intensity at the face of Mike. The golden light grew even brighter, yet in its very brilliance there was a purity and clarity that soothed their eyes.

Mike continued to look at his father with an affectionate smile on his face: then, suddenly, Jasper was looking at a mature and wonderfully beautiful soul. In a flash he realised that his son's life had been the final link in a long, long series of lives, and that it had been Jasper's privilege to have been his father while he was alive.

"At last you can see me as I really am," Mike greeted him. "Now you can see me with the dark glasses removed from your eyes. You are doubly my brother; for every human traveller is the brother of his fellow."

The joy that Jasper experienced flooded throughout the whole of his mind.

"But for the time being," continued Mike pleasantly, "I think we'll all feel more at ease if I retain the outward form of Mike!"

Jasper could only nod, inarticulate with happiness at the sight of this golden figure.

"Brother," said Mike, "we had to let you suffer your grief until it gave you clear, untroubled vision. And because *I* owe *you* many a karmic debt, we are going to aid each other. I will take you by the hand, brother, and show you exactly what you are: but for the time being, all I want you to realise is the fact that you and I are both sons of God, and it has come time for you to claim your birthright. This is of necessity your own responsibility. I can only aim your footsteps in the right direction. *You* must do the walking; nobody can do it for you. This has been true since mankind first stumbled onto the earth.

"Life is a steep mountain which we have to surmount before we can return to the Great One. Because I started up this path before you did, I have progressed a little further. This entitles me to be your mentor even when 'I also serve, who only stand and wait'.

"I see it still makes you self-conscious to see me as I really am. *But as I am, so are you! So never accept everything I say as infallible!* Always test it and prove it for yourself. Only thus will you truly learn what truth *is*; and once you understand how divine law operates, you will have mastered wisdom, for only by constantly testing and proving, can you convert experience to wisdom. Doubt as often as you like; test everything you can, you, and only *you*, will benefit.

"At the moment the laws of Nature have brought you to a point where life appears to have no meaning. Money seems to be the key — *if* you can show me a peaceful wealthy man! It might be more rewarding to look for a tramp who is hungry, cold and lonely. You're liable to find he's much more at peace with himself. But you will seldom find a plus without a minus nearby. Nor can you expect to find all the comforts of home in your mortal world. After all, it is only a classroom! Which may account for your frequent feeling that you are a laboratory white mouse, locked in a cage with no doors or windows.

"*Nature herself has brought you to this point.*

"You have a physical body. It repairs itself and runs itself. You have an emotional body. It controls the physical body. And you have a mental body. It perceives, absorbs and controls the other two.

"We will investigate these three bodies till you understand how to master them. Then, when they become perfect and precise tools, we shall lovingly seek out and find the Soul.

"For that is what you seek, my brother. That is your timeless quest!"

Part three

[*A further refining of Mike's vibrations enriches the relationship between father and son; for now an unusual loyalty and affection keeps the contact open. In the following passages, they are able to converse without the aid of Mrs. Merrington. N.L.*]

"I had better emphasise the nature of the three eternal laws before we go any further. These are the *Law of Love*, the *Law of the Group* and the *Law of the Land*.

"You have become aware of the 'repeating pattern' of reincarnation already, but now it is essential that you understand exactly *how* and *why* it operates. Only then will you realise that man could advance faster if he used greater caution; for he would be governed and not harassed by the consequences of his previous actions. Every action should be based on the result it will have on the do-er, the done-by, but most of all on whoever is fated to suffer most from its consequences.

"Hand in glove with this law, brother, is the Law of Love. Jesus asked man to love his neighbour as himself. This is better than asking man *not to hate* his neighbour as he hates himself; which he can do with small provocation! Restrain your impulses until you can trust them not to harm others. As long as your motives remain constructive, you are treating your neighbour as you would (or should) yourself, and divine law has no cause to hit you like a boomerang.

"This doesn't mean sitting back and letting things slide! Nearly two thousand years have passed since Jesus walked the earth, and mankind hasn't improved much yet. Do you ever consider what the world would be, if it had listened to his counsel? War would have been rendered impossible; most

75

disease would have been eliminated; and crime would not be an accepted part of society. All of us would be able to thrive under ideal conditions. Young souls would be encouraged to flower.

"Luckily for most of us, our Heavenly Father has all eternity in which to complete His project. Even so, He can only give us a choice of opportunities. He cannot make our decisions for us.

"It is with *you* that the choice rests. You can only apply His laws to your life as you feel you need them.

"This brings us to the Law of the Group. Not only must you gladly provide for your dependants; you must think of humanity itself in the same universal terms. Extend the negative of 'Never needlessly hurt anyone', to include the positive of 'How can I best serve the brotherhood of man?'

"The last of the laws by which you will have to abide, brother, is the Law of the Land; whether you think it makes good sense or bad. They are nevertheless the laws made by your brothers to suit your particular race on your particular planet. If you ever hope to live at peace with your community, you will have to respect its rules in your daily life. This doesn't mean allowing injustice to run amok. You must always work to right a wrong; but you *must* work from within the framework of the law of your particular land.

"Shall we recapitulate? Never commit yourself to an act that could result in a bad karmic debt to yourself.

"Take action only when you know that the results of your action will be harmless. Then aim to apply the result of that action to the benefit of your brothers.

"Always conform to the laws of the country you are in.

"If you operate within this framework, you must achieve peace within yourself.

"Most importantly I want you to assume the role of an *observer* from this moment onward.

"You must not only be a part of life *in* life, you must be *outside* life too, observing not only your own actions but everyone else's too. You'll pick up a first-rate education in very short order! Always remember that by observation you can best learn how the laws of the Great One operate. You will be able to satisfy yourself of their validity. Whether we like it or not, they operate daily in every life on the surface of the globe. Only an idiot would disobey a law, once he knows it exists for his benefit!

"The first thing you'll notice as you begin to refine your life pattern, is that you start getting into trouble everywhere . . . with your family, with the authorities, with every conceivable link you have ever made with another human being. *Take this as the gratifying proof that it was high time for your life to change!*

"When your approach complies with the three great Laws, your mind (which may have been neither very positive nor very negative) suddenly swings to an uncharacteristically negative extreme. This sets up an upsurge of *all* negative forces strong enough to influence your fortunes in life.

"You will find that those who know and love you best will now become exasperated by you. Up to now they were probably able to predict your response to any given set of circumstances. Now your thought processes only confound them. Most of them will ask you what the devil has gone wrong with you. You can indulge in no outraged protests when this occurs. Protest *silently*, and weigh the situation very carefully before you make another move. Even the expenditure of that caution can create enough energy to tilt your polarity into its negative extreme!

"Take heart. It is necessary to travel by night before you can fully appreciate day. This is how you change gear. You travel at the negative level so that you can proceed from it to the highest point of your comprehension. If you were to consult a clairvoyant, he would be able to detect the change in your auric colours after you have changed gear, and he could assess their improvement in clarity and purity.

"It matters little which world you happen to be frequenting — there are seven planes of existence, and each plane is more positive than the one below it — self-discipline will always raise you above the negative vibrations of emotion at the astral level, and adjust you to the vibrations of the mind at the more rarified mental level.

"When you have progressed far enough to emerge at the mental level, your previous life shrinks down into its negative aspect, and all hell breaks loose! You will find yourself becoming emotionally unstable. Necessarily so: for you are already operating on a mental wave-length. Previously, you had been 'programmed' to operate on the astral, or emotional, wave-length. But while you are gearing yourself to the mental world, your emotion will take the bit in its teeth and you may think you've been kicked by a runaway cart-horse.

"Knowing the real why and wherefore, however, gives you a ninety-nine per cent chance of victory. When you *know* your emotions are going to give you a hard time, you watch them like a hawk; and the mere fact that you are watching them keeps them somewhat to heel.

"The Great One safeguards his children every inch of the way, so don't waste valuable time on false fears as you mountain-climb your way up His path. But there is one point you had better remember! As His son, you are now taking your welfare into your own hands, and therefore it is vital that you adopt a dispassionate approach, and see yourself as others see you.

"I know how hard it is to play the observer when one is at the centre of one's own finite world. What can possibly be more important than what is going to happen to oneself? But you *do* have to stand aside and look at yourself as just another member of your particular species. Forget your personal likes and dislikes. Forget the need for self-preservation at any cost. Knock off the green glasses that have glued themselves to your eyes.

"*I'm trying to persuade you to hold out your arms and objectively embrace the whole of humanity!*

"One of the most inimical taboos in society must now be bearded in its den. The question of sex in modern life; the biological difference between man and woman. The *practical* answer to the problem is so easily resolved that I hope you won't consider it trite: just remember that the Great One knows what is best for his children! I assure you that there is no better place in which to train the reflexes than amid the hurly-burly of everyday family life, where the challenge is to identify with humanity as a whole, not to elect yourself the only perfect pebble on the beach.

"An individual fish in the middle of a shoal of fishes concerns himself solely with the direction in which his brother fishes are going, and his only fear is that he will be left behind. By the same token, the shoal is an entity that divides its time into feeding and travelling, thus fulfilling its primordial function. I'm sure the logic of such a life-pattern would be incomprehensible to any one lone member of the shoal, who is therefore better off not trying to bite off more than he can chew. You too must learn to trust humanity as a whole, rather than your own fat hope that you are the only fish who knows all the answers. It will make it easier for you to understand what *is* and what is *not* essential to your progress as an embryonic god about to enter the Olympian incubator.

"So far so good. Now let's get down to specifics. Essentially we have to try and understand what makes you personally tick with the maximum efficiency. The best way to do that is to find out *what* you are in the overall scheme of things.

"You are a very complex mechanism, in case you didn't know it. You consist of a physical body; an electrical or etheric body to energise the physical body; and an astral or emotional body. The etheric body is essentially the launching-pad beneath the physical, and therefore part of it. Remove its launching-pad and the physical body dies. Over and above all that, you have a mental body. Finally, at the hub of the entire composite, is your immortal soul.

"The *mental* body must resolve itself before it can perceive its kinship to the physical, the etheric and the astral. Then all of a sudden it says to itself: 'Here is my mind, here are my emotions, and here is my body. Who, if anyone, is seeing them through my eyes? What is the sum total of all my components?' Then that entity realises that it is in fact an immortal soul: a Prodigal Son utilising a series of bodies in order to return intact to the protection of the Eternal Father.

"Look at the lives of the people you love, and who are therefore the most important to you. You will see that every man's life breaks down into five important phases. From the hour of his birth, the incarnating soul has been learning to occupy the new shape he has found himself stuck with. Until the age of seven, he is preoccupied by the problem of how to gain attention to himself *and* how to co-ordinate his limbs!

"Between the ages of seven and fourteen, he starts to develop emotions; he starts to experience love. And he starts to develop a temperament!

"At fourteen, he faces the crisis of adolescence. The *emotional* body begins to take control of the *physical* body.

"From the age of fourteen, the intensity increases until his mind awakens at twenty-one.

"From twenty-one to twenty-eight the mind advances until he begins to realise that there is more to life than he first thought.

"From the age of twenty-eight, the *mental* body takes over and learns how to adjust itself to the lower *emotional* and *physical* bodies.

"By the age of thirty-five, this process should be complete (if it is ever going to be). The man is now *mentally orientated*.

"From thirty-five to forty-two, he becomes aware of something else in life. This is due to the probing of his soul, which is now seeking means to control the mind.

"From forty-two to forty-nine this process intensifies. During this period, the man becomes aware of the presence of his soul.

"From forty-nine to fifty-six, he realises that there is much more to life than selfishly 'eating high on the hog'. He begins to wonder whether he has actually achieved anything in his life, or whether it was 'all vanity and led but to the grave'.

"The conclusion is reached between the age of fifty-six and sixty-three. Either he decides to serve out his sentence to the bitter end, in the hope that it will finally solve the riddle of existence, or he elevates himself to our Golden Plane. He may go through an interminable array of lifetimes, but the pattern will always fall into these seven year cycles.

"With that in mind, let us try to co-ordinate the physical body, the emotional body and the mental body into one beautiful streamlined instrument. It is this instrument that will enable us to emulate Jesus and find the essential divinity within ourselves.

"Your finite world is divided into kingdoms: the mineral kingdom, the vegetable, the animal and the human kingdoms. To learn how our multiple bodies react to each of these, we will have to begin at the beginning. The finite world in which you now exist. along with all the other worlds in this galaxy, was made of tangible energy: in other words, vibration.

"God in the very beginning was alone in a vast sea of thought. Nothing tangible had as yet been created. I don't claim to know the origin of God or the end of God! I am only trying to give you a reasonable hypothesis, so that you can follow me more clearly.

"Let us assume that God is omnipotent, omniscient and omnipresent. Seeing that He did not exist, why did He want to get an idea of Himself, apart from Himself? Yet He did. He split off from himself, sixty-three thousand million sparks. Then, by a mighty effort of will, He ripped a rent in the primeval void and forcibly widened two points of tension until they created a gap in that void. A magnetic interplay sprang up between them, through which the universes and galaxies were able to manifest.

"As they solidified, those millions of sparks were also able to manifest as concrete matter. They will never be able to reverse the process and return to the source from whence they came, until they are self-reliant enough to undergo the process themselves.

"Rest assured that then, and *only* then, will they be able to comprehend that they exist. In other words, only God knows and sees and understands just who and why He is.

"*All* matter is vibration. Water is a liquid; you can hold it in a glass in front of you and look at it; you can see it, you can touch it, sometimes you can even smell it. If you apply heat to that water, you speed up the vibration and it turns into steam. If you slow down the vibration, you turn the water into solid ice. Ice and water and steam all consist of the same components; but as the vibration speeds up or slows down, they take on three entirely different attributes. The *rate of vibration* of the molecules of hydrogen oxide, which comprise water, is the *sole differentiating factor.* Ice, the solid; water, the fluid; and steam, the gas; all are quite independent of each other at the physical level; all are still one and the same thing; all are differentiated solely by the rate of molecular vibration. *The whole of this universe is based on this principle. Everything is vibration.*

"The Oriental philosophers hold that everything is light. Jesus himself said that everything is light. And this interpretation of light simply refers to its rate of molecular vibration, which, in its highest form, we cannot perceive.

"You must also bear in mind that while you are a mortal spirit in an animal body, your only contact with the world around you is via your five senses: feeling, touch, sight, hearing and taste. If none of those senses were available to you, good brother, if you couldn't see or hear; you would be a non-organic vegetable! We perceive the world around us *only* through those five senses.

"Can you say that X-rays don't exist, simply because you can't perceive them? You know they *do* exist, when you see the X-ray plates which enable the doctor to set a broken bone. And yet you can't *feel* an X-ray. You can't *touch* it. You can't *smell* it. None of your senses can alert you to the presence of an X-ray. Yet it exists. You have incontrovertible proof of that.

"Not long ago there was quite a flap in a Belgian hospital because two radium needles which had been used in the treatment of cancer disappeared down the sluices along with the diseased tissues. Nobody could smell, feel, taste, touch or see the radiation from those needles. But as soon as their loss was discovered, the doctor simply walked around with a geiger counter until the noise of the radiation directed them to the drain which concealed the needles. None of their human senses could have detected the existence of that radium; but fortunately that didn't alter the fact that radium exists!

"So don't necessarily discredit a thing *only* because you cannot examine it with your naked eye! Continue to evolve, and you will develop extra-sensory powers which will enable you to perceive even the most sensitive wave-bands of vibration.

"Well, to pick up where we left off: We have this force, God, creating sixty-three million sparks out of His own energy and then plunging them into the world of matter . . . . a world, remember, that only came into being when two magnetic poles were forced apart; a positive pole and a negative pole. In the magnetic field between these two poles, the vibration slowed down until it congealed into searing hot gases. As more energy escaped, so did it solidify into the planetary system as it exists today. This new energy field attracted the myriad sparks of divinity, dragging them to the bottom of the slowest, thickest matter.

"It is the difference in the speed of vibration that distinguishes one physical state from its neighbour — remember the ice, the water and the steam? — and as mortal life is locked in at the very dense level of matter, it will have to work its *own* way back to its divine source.

"This is what I really meant when I talked about the steep mountain pathway back to God.

"The earth-energy imprisoned between the two divergent poles splits itself into four separate kingdoms; the mineral, where the rate of vibration is slowest; the vegetable, where the rate of vibration is somewhat faster; the animal, where the rate is faster still; and finally the human kingdom, where spirit first found itself stifling in inanimate matter. Gradually, as evolution affected these separate zones, the neutrons and electrons were forced to rearrange themselves: and when some of them became radio-active, the life-force evolved in the *mineral* kingdom.

"The life-force then expanded to encompass the *vegetable* kingdom. Here I want to make it clear to you that the atom, when it finally achieves radio-activity, radiates the sum-total of its energy and then slowly reverts back, inert as lead; but the molecule that is able to rise to the vegetable kingdom is assimilated by a root, and becomes part of a plant. In other words, an organised entity has evolved, having drawn on all the various minerals to bring about a new pattern of existence. When the plant is thus affected, it becomes a new life-form independent of its antecedents, and a *soul* is brought into being; even though it is not yet able to choose its own habitat. It has to take whatever the wind and rain and sun choose to bring it, and it lies at their mercy.

"It next graduates to the *animal* kingdom; where it is able to develop a sense of individuality. Now it can move away from surroundings that don't suit it. The animal can shelter itself under a nearby tree, rather than expire from the heat of the sun. The wider variety of choice enables the life-force unit to command that much more of its environment.

"Now the third great step takes place. The animal is becoming a thinking, coherent entity. It still tends to travel in groups; but each animal, being an individual, is an entity in itself. When the animal becomes enough of an individual *to become aware of itself,* it begins to select its company, experiences pleasure and fear, and flees from danger. And when it comprehends its basic needs, it will begin to simplify the process of catching its prey.

"The *mineral* kingdom is comparable to our body; it is inert matter. Left to its own devices, it would be too inert to know that it existed! The *astral* kingdom exists in our emotional body. It has no ties with the *vegetable* kingdom, where life can only respond to the light in which it grows and flourishes.

"The *animal* kingdom is able to use its mind to preserve itself. It can select the food that will keep it alive. Doesn't this make it part of the *mental* kingdom too? And doesn't that complete the parallel between our three bodies and the three kingdoms just below us on the evolutionary scale?

"It never hurts to appreciate just how closely the human kingdom, which you consciously inhabit, connects you to the elements from which you came, even though aeons of mortal time are involved.

"Small, sentient forms of life are still evolving through these three kingdoms; first into the animal and finally into the human kingdom, where they will acquire souls.

"The elephant and the porpoise are two of the most highly evolved intelligences in the animal kingdom. Isn't it reasonable to suppose that each of them has a perfect right to evolve into the human kingdom and inhabit a human soul?

"Think of the times you've watched a man eating like a pig, or fighting with the courage of a lion, or boasting the total recall of an elephant. The similies might well be factual! As a matter of fact, I can tell you that they usually *are*! Does that help you to appreciate just what *you* are? — the complex result of a long evolutionary process!

"Bravo, good brother! You're adopting the attitude of the dispassionate observer in fine style! And when you finally polarise yourself on the mental plane, the imbalance between the astral and the mental plane will regain its equilibrium. This will have the further effect of promoting your soul to a *place above the mental plane*. This in turn will activate a negative balance which must then be converted to positive; which will give you a rough idea of the uproar that's going on in all your three higher bodies at the same time! The soul plane is developing a negative bias; the mental is veering more and more towards the positive; while the astral is sinking lower and lower over the horizon. Do you wonder that your life-pattern is coming apart at the seams?

"But don't give up the ship. Your built-in self preservation will eventually bring harmony to these three discordant levels.

"The first action station you will have to defend, (and I can see it happening now within you) will be the scene of extreme confusion. This will manifest itself, more and more strongly, as a lack of logical reason until it finally exposes itself as common-or-garden *fear*.

"It is a fear you can easily conquer, as long as you understand what brought it about. Eventually it will *have* to work itself out. Meanwhile, however, it will do its best to manifest at every opportunity. You will begin to doubt whether you really know right from wrong. You will certainly feel you shouldn't have stuck your neck so far out. And you will ruefully recall how happy you were before it all began!

"But always remember, good brother, that advancement *always* means forsaking the old; which explains why your normal equilibrium has now become the deck of the listing Titanic. As you begin to doubt yourself, you doubt the world around you. You will be quite in your rights if you even doubt *my* sanity when I encourage you to press on, regardless!

"But as you begin to regain control of your equilibrium, you will realise that you are making vital progress; and as you *have* to go through with it now, good brother, why not decide to enjoy it? I'll repeat myself; learn to enjoy it! There's nothing to be gained by letting fear clog your reasoning processes. Whenever you feel uncertain, go back and re-examine the cause in your mind, and find out exactly *how* valid it was. It's a funny thing, but when you get a firm grip of a misgiving, and expose it to the light of day, it diminishes down to the evanescent wisp of nothing that it always was. It cannot survive being examined by your mind, because in cold hard fact it has never existed; it was only an hallucination born of self-doubt. This is the time for you to remember that you are a composite being, with four energy bodies that must eventually vibrate in unison.

"For the last five or six centuries, you have been living at a rate of vibration that devours your astral, or emotional, energy. Life is a circular staircase of ever-evolving self-perception. If you live for five hundred years on an astral plane, the astral body is bound to develop a measure of self-awareness, quite independent of the indwelling soul.

"Why should it surprise you then, that when you begin elevating the vibrations of that very potent body of yours, the astral refuses to surrender the little modicum of independence it has been able to gain? It is going to fight for its very existence, good brother! And *this* is the reason for the doubts that flood your mind. The astral has been a good and faithful saddle-horse which is now being put out to grass because a new and much more powerful horse is being groomed to replace it in the stable. Of course it wants to object; and it does! The best way to control it is to make sure that every order it receives is correctly given and is absolutely necessary for the ultimate good of all concerned. Once these doubts are silenced, you can begin to see the wood in spite of the trees.

"If, however, you feel that too many doubts have pressed on you for you to separate the main trouble-maker from all its cohorts, forget the whole business, good brother! Go out into the fresh air and occupy yourself with hard labour — *any* kind of hard labour, dig a hole a yard deep and a yard square, and then leave it there until the next time your doubts assail you. Then go and fill it back in!

"Or, if you prefer, run for two or three miles, so that you exhaust your physical body. But be prepared to run until the sweat pours off you in buckets! You will increase the power-supply from the etheric electrical main which services your mortal body. When it is forced to operate at maximum power, it *forces* energy from the astral body above it. Whereupon your doubts disappear. They must. There is no energy left to operate them. Exhaust your body, take a hot shower, put on fresh pyjamas, and go to bed. You will sleep like a baby. This is emergency-crash procedure, to be used when things seem to have got beyond control. And it works, good brother, it really works!

"This issue of fear and doubt can also be diagnosed as 'nervous exhaustion', or expanded into 'I have just flipped my wig prior to going bonkers!' It simply means that *none* of us, brother, is skilled enough to keep in the saddle when a chronic upheaval has stampeded his serial bodies, above *and* below the conscious level.

"Another thing I would like you to do (even if it upsets your mode of living somewhat) is to get out of bed shortly before sunrise and throw open your window. Watch the rising of the sun until it has crested the horizon. I want you to enjoy the beauty of the dawn colours, the ever changing hues of the clouds. I want you to watch the shadowy hills suddenly dissolve into the brilliant hues of day. (If the day happens to be overcast and rainy and you can see no glimmer of the sun, recall the sunrise of the day before, and re-live it in your mind.) Most of all I want you to open up your heart, and bask in the peace and quiet with which our Father rewards each and every one of us, even if only a lucky few of us appreciate it.

"Open the doors to your heart and give Him your loving thanks. Within a moment, the love of our beloved Father will flow back to you a hundredfold and you will realise that even here, in mortal terms, you are indeed His son.

"When you have mastered this simple form of meditation, you will always find release from the petty troubles all around you. All you will have to do is to sit quietly in some secluded spot, and re-create the tranquil peace you knew when you welcomed that perfect dawn.

"You will also have helped to integrate those four jittery sub-bodies you possess, even at their most mutinous. This 'peace beyond understanding' can filter through you until it fills you with serenity. It is then that you can open the way to positive gain at the *mental* level.

"Thereafter, good brother, you can investigate the world around you with the clear thinking that reflects a properly balanced intuition.

"Now let's get on with your four sub-bodies and see how they correlate to your conscious ego. Good brother, if you are sensible enough to regard your body as a temple built for a son of God to inhabit, isn't it only fair that it remains a credit to the Original Owner, to whom it must eventually be returned? When you wake on the mental plane, you will realise that you *are* and *always have been* a son of God. Will you feel that you always behaved as such, even when you were in the cocoon-stage on earth; half defunct caterpillar, and half butterfly-to-be?

"Whoever hopes to claim his birthright in the presence of our Father must follow His road. So, good brother, we are definitely going somewhere! We are definitely going to produce effects which may well be mind boggling when we first perceive them. But as soon as we understand what they are and why they are happening, they will no longer startle. We can only welcome them.

"So sustain your faith, good brother; in yourself and in the Path. It has lasted since Adam trod the earth, and it is as tangible as it is eternal. Seek the wherewithal to become a creator as your Father would wish.

"Hand-in-glove with all your confusion is a paralysing sense of loneliness. This is a direct result of the altered course of your polarity. Confronted by the positive mental polarity, the once-positive astral polarity has begun to founder. Because you are in trouble with all who cross your path, the strain affects your nervous system, and loneliness will predominate until you eventually take yourself in hand.

"This forsaken loneliness is not something new. It has been suffered by every brother determined enough to set foot upon the Path. He must of necessity regress five miles into the negative, in order to advance six miles into the positive. As you are now entering the Great Brotherhood of Man, or the 'Brotherhood of Light', you will plough your way into an isolated bank of loneliness before you can claim equality with the emancipated company of which you are now a junior member.

"One begins the ascent of the Path under the chaotic conditions caused by the switch in polarity; so one will be overwhelmed by loneliness. Be prepared for this, good brother. You are lonely, you will stand alone. Nobody (so you will think) understands the crisis you find yourself in.

"This is good. Before a pilot is trusted with large commercial aircraft, he must succeed in a series of solo flights.

"Before *you* can qualify as one of the great Brotherhood of

Light, you too must learn to take your life in your hands and mould it until it responds with perfect obedience. When that happens, your suffocating sense of desolation will be replaced by the companionship of the Brotherhood; which in its turn will lead to the warmth and protection of your Father.

"The ultimate goal of this Path is re-union with God Eternal, not the complete annihilation of yourself. It is akin to a drop of water placed in the ocean. It merges with the whole of that ocean, and yet it still retains its independence; you can always take that drop out of the ocean again.

"This intense loneliness is only the necessary separation of you from the meaningless ebb and flow of mortal life. As you progress along the Path, you will learn how to blend yourself into your surroundings. *From that moment on, you will never again be lonely.*

"But at *this* stage, good brother, loneliness is essential to your development. Accept it with good cheer, because it is living proof that you have risen above the confines of the common herd. That alone is enough to make you feel you now live in an empty void.

"*Try to think of humanity as the plankton on the surface of a seething murky sea.* Along its shores, a benign species of spirit intently observes the dark surface of the water. Whenever one of the dim emerging souls accepts the responsibility of its own destiny, it reveals its presence to the watchers by giving off an erratic little flicker of light.

"*As soon as the watchers see that glimmer, they pluck the soul free of the seething mass of humanity, and place its feet on the upward Path.* It is at this very moment, as the soul feels itself separated from its brethren, that its loneliness hits home with all its force. Rejoice in it, good brother! Be happy, for this is the proof positive that you truly are a son of God, not a dab of mortal clay!

"Later on, helpers more potent and powerful than I will assist in your development; but to 'start the ball rolling' you had to make an unaided effort to lift yourself out of the mass. Only thus could we become aware of you.

"And you have only to look back at that seething mass from whence you came, to see that even there the Laws of the Great

One operate continually, swirling the sluggish waters too and fro, until one or another of the embryonic souls begins to pulsate.

"This is the essence of the unhurried evolutionary process of nature which advances mankind; and at this stage I am content to measure the development of mankind against the four kingdoms that confront it in nature.

"There have been many civilisations in the past, through all of which man developed. He first inhabited his 'multiple body' in the Lemurian civilisation, when the indwelling soul appropriated the functions of the body and learned to exercise its five senses, thus to prepare them for the world of incarnation. By 'functions of the body' I refer to the senses of sight, hearing, smell, touch and feeling. With the use of these five senses, the body came into line with the great Cosmic Law of Ebb and Flow.

"Then the Atlantean civilisation arose. It was here that the soul learnt to control the astral body.

"At the present time you are a cog in the Aryan civilisation. It is now that mankind will begin to obtain control over the mental body.

"In the civilisation that will supersede this one, there will be a conscious coordination of the three bodies man has developed so far.

"Now do you see how, by separating yourself from the bulk of humanity, you have shot out so far ahead that you have even out-stripped its most august leaders? So I put it to you that your sense of 'untouchability' is, in effect, wonderful confirmation that you are proceeding up the right Path!

"Which brings us back to the *Law of Polar Opposites*. I want you to regard this Law from an objective point of view, as though you were standing aside and observing it as a bystander. And this is as good a time as any to deal with the question of Evil.

"When human genesis took place, the Eternal Father created a point of crisis by wrenching two centres apart in the primeval substance, so that magnetic forces could come into play in the void between them. I have used the word *magnetic* to dramatise the intense rate of vibration caused by the pulling apart of the poles in the primeval void. All subsequent manifestation resulted from it. Where one pole is negative and the other is positive, our chance of survival depends on our ability to keep to the narrow, narrow path in the middle zone, where the positive and the negative cancel each other out, leaving only the zone of neutrality.

"One day science will discover that the basic value of the amino acids is not confined to their use as the basic building-block of the proteins which constitute 90% of the blood and 80% of the tissue. When harnessed to the enzyme, the amino acids cause such a marked increase in the vibratory rate of the whole system that they lift the awareness of each cell up to the realms of the astral. When all the cells have achieved an equal boost in vibration, the awareness of the body is heightened until the astral can actually be perceived. Tangible evidence of the astral dimension at the physical level accounts for such phenomena as apports and materialisations. But a clear majority of the body's cells must be able to achieve this heightened rate— hence the Oriental insistence on a pure mind, which will automatically eliminate the low-vibration molecule. The whole driving force of Buddhism derives from this fact. What else are the four noble truths and the eight-fold way? And by the eight-fold use of sane perspective in thought, word and deed, we purify the vibratory rate of the entire system.

" 'All we are is the result of what we have thought.'

"The mind can wholly control the body by preventing the vital amino acids from undergoing an animal break-down process. Instead of ejecting them from the system as urea, the mind can redirect them to combine with the enzymes until they achieve the correct speed of vibration. When the cells of the brain are likewise affected, perception of the astral by the sensory organs is possible. The uninitiated, who stumble onto this level simply by living a decent life, see and hear foggy echoes of the real thing. These can only 'go bump in the night' and fill them with fears for their sanity! *The astral is ever the great deluder, but it will always reluctantly surrender its secrets to the illumined mind.* The key to the whole process is simply vibration; so much so that the material, astral, mental, and spiritual planes can *all* co-exist in the selfsame area; yet the lower is ever oblivious of the higher level.

"A lethal toxin can be created simply by slowing down the vibratory rate of the cell involved. Once he has gained control of the tempo of the cells, a man can guzzle deadly poisons with impunity. All he has to do is speed up the vibration in his mind, ever remembering that astral matter responds directly and instantly to thought. This is the 'ye shall move mountains' prediction in a slightly different context.

"*And this is the stony upward Path.*

"To find this Path, you must be able to immunize yourself to the positive, and then emerge from it successfully enough to immunize yourself to the negative. Then, and *only* then, will you know when these two forces are exactly balanced. That, good brother, in the simplest possible terms, is the *only* way you can distinguish good from evil.

"Neither underestimate nor overestimate the power of evil. Good and evil are variations of the same vibrations, and both exist, regardless of your ego or mine. They are vibrations created by our Father; so as long as I employ a natural force for *good* I am safe within my natural boundaries.

"Let us take the hypothetical case of a man who employs that selfsame force to promote *evil*. Does this turn the force itself into something evil? (This is a distinction I would encourage you to make.) The force, surely, is not to be blamed at all. The soul manipulating the force can either manipulate it for good *or* for evil: as a result of which the Law of Retribution moves into action. If you manipulate a force for *good*, you will be rewarded in like coin; manipulate it for *evil*, and you will still get as good as you gave!

"This is the divine pattern, and it cannot be double-talked by a plausible liar. So never regard any of our Father's powers as good or evil. They are all impartial. I want you to forget your cut-and-dried concept of evil and realise that *there is no such thing as a force of evil.*

"There *is* such a thing as a force being *used* for evil: but even then, the force itself is not evil.

"I am not denying the existence of the Black Brotherhood. It is permitted to exist. These are souls who exploit the energy of the cosmos for their own selfish ends, and they turn a deaf ear to its effect on friend or foe. But they are held down by a built-in brakedrum. They can never hope to progress further than the mastery of mental control.

"The soul, being evanescently good, cannot partake of an act which might result in evil. The Black Brotherhood may become expert at mastering the natural forces in their physical, emotional, and mental bodies; *but they cannot progress beyond that point.* Those of them who have tried to progress beyond the mental stage, have re-activated their immortal souls as well; whereupon an internal conflict wages between the positive soul and the negative mind, and the perpetrator is flung back to the bottom of the ladder of evolution. This entails a long and dismal uphill climb, in which the soul must work itself up again from elementary matter to regained self-respect.

"There is no need to fear or pity the 'evil' Brotherhood; only remember that they are still your mis-directed brothers, even when they put fatuous self-aggrandisement ahead of mutual salvation.

"To exorcise any 'evil' thing that may have harried you in the past, good brother, send it love. Send it your blessing. Send it your deep heartfelt prayer that it will evolve into the perfect soul your Father intended it to be before it lost its way.

"This is the mightiest weapon you have in your hands. If it is too old in evil to be reformed at one fell swoop, you will at least embarrass it to such an extent that it will put the greatest distance between itself and you!

"Your thought of love is positive; and *every* positive thought that impinges upon a negative thought *invalidates a portion of it;* it is not long before it can no longer exist.

"It is a bright and sunny morning. Elizabeth, a charming nineteen year-old, is walking down a freshly sprinkled street. Everything is clean, everything is fresh and new. There is a spring in her step. Yet on her forehead is a small worried frown.

"Elizabeth is about to come face to face with one of the greatest tragedies of your polite society, good brother. In forty-eight hours she is to marry the man she dearly loves. John is a young architect. On the threshold of his profession, he is the proud possessor of a reasonable income. The future for these two is expected to be very, very rosy. She is the confidential secretary to the managing director of a large conglomerate, which gives her a good income in her own right. Their combined incomes will allow them to build the home of their dreams. Why, then, the small worried frown?

"She has been brought up to think of sex as something that is 'not quate nace'. She has been told that its problems are best left alone until she has wed the man she loves. Then, at the touch of some hifalutin' magic wand, everything will work out perfectly. But she is intuitively aware that when they share the first night of their honeymoon together, she will have to do a right-about-face and forget everything she has been taught. How can she possibly be feminine and yielding, understanding and comforting; and yet sexy withal? This horrible, repulsive bugaboo she has been warned against so repeatedly, this 'keep yourself pure until you yield to the man you love', is bringing its chickens home to roost, even though Elizabeth was one of the lucky few who went to a school where a certain amount of guarded biology was taught. She *did* know what sex was, she knew why there were two opposite sexes and how they differed, but of the natural function of sex in her life, she remained completely ignorant. Good brother, what chance of success does that marriage have? She completely ignorant, he likewise?

"Sex is fundamentally a sober sacrament. Indeed, it is a microcosm of the creation of all life on this planet. Yet mankind, in its passion for double standards and whited sepulchres, has smothered the subject like a sow rolling onto its litter in a pigsty.

"The result is mental and astral aberrations by the trillion.

"There are three aspects of sex that man must accept for what they are. The first is physical sex *per se*, the naked and unashamed means by which the human species reproduces itself. The second occurs when you raise the energy of the lower triad so that it combines with the higher triad to stimulate the heart centre. The third is when the pineal and pituitary centres (the first of which lies between the eyebrows, the second at the centre of the skull) have become so stimulated that they indulge in mutual interplay until this, in turn, awakens the responses of the soul.

"I have told you how our Father created a point of tension out of the primeval void, thereby creating a vast magnetic embryo which resulted in the creation of the cosmos. Everything was on an inconceivably large scale, from a mortal's eye view; nevertheless, this set the pattern for all creation; a pattern best described as the operation of the Law of Polar Opposites.

"I don't mean the Arctic or the Antarctic. I am talking about a positive pole and a negative pole. When we eventually come to the creation of man on the earth, we find that He simultaneously created woman; man being negative and woman being positive.

"When we compare the physical body of the male with that of the female, there is only an infinitesmal difference between them; and even that is confined to the reproductive organs. You would merely have to 'externalise' the female reproductive organs to turn her into a male. On all the higher spiritual planes, their bodies are identical; so it is obvious that these two opposites at the physical level were only created for the convenience of incarnating spirits. Man and woman only identify themselves as opposites in order to stand surety for the new life seeking admission to the physical world.

"This is when the hornet in the woodpile appears, good brother! Consider the vanity with which we devote so much care and attention to our bodies. We call them our temples. We protest that they are all we have; that if they should break down, we would collapse in chaos.

"The hyperbole is too vainglorious.

"We come nearer to home if we take the car you bought three years ago. It is showing signs of wear and tear, besides which, you were beginning to get fed up with it anyway. You originally bought the car for the purpose of travelling from one spot on the map to another; and by riding instead of walking, you saved yourself a great deal of time and trouble. As soon as it developed problems, you traded it in without compunction.

"Your own internal works have much in common with your ageing car, good brother. You only regard your body as important because, without it, there would be no 'you' on your mundane planet. From where we observe you, your soul is your only permanent fixture; your body is simply a convenient mackintosh you borrowed during your stay on a very impermanent plane.

"I hope this also enables you to understand why nobody here sheds so much as a crocodile tear when cyclones and earthquakes decimate your populations. We are accustomed to welcoming all the participants back here; even when they return a hundred thousand at a time!

"To the fledgling soul, it is of course a hardship when its experience on the earth is terminated too abruptly; but even the fledgling soul is wise and patient in vital things, so it is quite content to wait here until a suitable flesh-body becomes available, enabling it to reincarnate.

"Nobody at our end gives the matter another thought!

"So for all the weeping and wailing and gnashing of teeth that obscures and distorts the issue in your world, up here we regard a lethal phenomenon as one more creak in the cog of evolution and we give it our complete cooperation. We, after all, are the only *bona fide* receiving station for the dispossessed soul.

"So, good brother, never make the mistake of thinking that your Father in all His mercy has forgotten a soul on the earth plane. He could no more forget one of His children than disappear from the scene Himself.

"Jesus made this clear by his emphasis on the death of the sparrow.

"It is the attitude we all share here; for we are too far away to debate the pros and cons of being the proud possessor of a human body, or even question whether it is important or not. It is only good sense, after all, to take good care of your body while you rent it. If you don't, it can easily refuse to serve you. In which case, back you'll come to us. Back here, you will be impatient to get into a brand new earth-body as quickly as possible so that you can add cubits to the experience you are building. But the body, even yours at its most personable, is still nothing more than a vehicle! If you want it to serve you well, groom it as you would a thoroughbred horse in your stable. Ill treat it, and you will have to incarnate *again and again* before your necessary quota of experience is achieved.

"The physical sex aspect may be old-hat to you, good brother, after living half your life in your own corner of the finite world. It is, after all, a purely animal drive dedicated to

96

the propagation of the species. The psychologist Freud defined its value very well when he divided the field of human activity into three arenas; the arena of *work*, the arena of *play* and the arena of *sex*. Mortal man has to function effectively in every one of these arenas if he hopes to maintain his balance. If he functions in play and in sex, but not in work, he will very soon be vulnerable to mental and emotional disturbance. Likewise, that man who works and who plays, but sublimates sex, will find himself up a neurotic creek. You have to function normally in all three fields before you are eligible for your sanity test.

"The only way to deal with physical sex *per se* is to treat it exactly as you treat the other basic needs of your body — the need to eat, the need to drink and the need to sleep. Keep them under the control of your mind. Never allow the tail to wag the dog!

"You know perfectly well that if you eat too much, you will become fat. If you allow the mind to referee, it will cut down the intake and control the greed. Similarly, the mind must control the taste for physical sex, so that it only operates at the proper time and the proper place. The urge itself is basic and must be met, but let it be the servant of moderation!

"Because the male species is of a dominant *negative* polarity and the female is of a *positive* polarity, the male tends to think of himself as superior, not only in physical strength, but at the mental level. Too bad for him! The male is negative, and when I say this I mean that his whole organism is totally negative.

"As I said before, you only have to externalise the reproductive organs of the female and you will have a male. Astrally and mentally, the woman is the stronger because she is of a positive polarity; it is she who preserves new-born life until it can fend for itself.

"Now, let us take a closer look at the etheric body underlying the physical body. The *etheric* body looks like a network of small golden-gleaming threads; these are the energy sources. Along the spine are seven glowing centres. Starting from the base of the spine, the first centre is the basal. Above that is the sacral, situated roughly at the centre of the pelvis. Next is the solar plexus; above that is the heart centre; above the heart centre is the throat centre. Then comes the centre between the eyebrows (once the location of the third eye); last comes the head centre.

"The fourth centre, the heart, is the key centre, the *balancer.* It is necessary for the lower three centres to look like swirling, glowing points, all burning at the same intensity. Then the three upper centres must be coordinated into a like activity.

"When the lower triangle and the higher triangle are balanced in energy, the heart centre can then bring them together and superimpose the upper on the lower.

"This, good brother, is the mystical marriage that you will have to experience, for it results in the perfection of man within himself. A blazing white light illuminates the heart centre as the two triads merge. Only after this process has taken place, both in the man *and* in the woman, will there be the proper union of the son and the daughter of the Father. (It is here that such as I guide those lower on the evolutionary scale by talking to them until we can begin to understand them. When I say that, good brother, I do not mean *interfere*! I mean we *only* guide them.)

"Be warned in advance of the following hazards. The centre at the *base* of the spine is known in Oriental literature as the raising of the *Kundalini,* or Serpent of Fire. Let me advise you at once, good brother; *never* provoke, in any manner whatever, the Kundalini! Its forced development invariably ends in disaster for the person concerned! It belongs in its own place in the perfect scheme that our Father set before us, so let us walk this Path properly; let us not shortcut the sequence of experiences we must undergo. In other words, to combine the highest centre with the lowest, you must exercise the will to succeed, the will to learn and the will to know. When you have done that, a beam of light will link the highest centre to the lowest, and they will all begin to glow.

"The next centre, the *sacral,* which governs the reproductive organs, is energised by the *third eye*; and from there, good brother, we turn to the *solar plexus* centre, the source of the sub-sonscious mind. This we animate by linking it with the *throat* centre. These two centres also respond as you involve yourself deeper in self-betterment. When the lower three centres eventually rotate as brightly as the upper three, the fourth centre, the *heart* centre, will merge with the upper and lower triad; and into that fulfulled human life, the all-understanding love of our Father will manifest. You will now be a perfected human being. You can identify yourself as negative.

98

"When you realise that your perfected female counterpart is the positive pole, your two souls merge and a deeper sense of consciousness will arise . . . the awareness of yourselves as sons of God . . . a full awareness of the whole of creation around you . . . . then indeed, good brother, do you achieve the ultimate unification of the two poles!

"It is only when this *union of the opposites* triumphs that the final barriers dissolve; for after this mystical union, the two can separate, each to discover his own immortality. He is now *she* and she is now *he*; and both are at one with the fulfilled concept of the Brotherhood of Man.

"This is the true, the ultimate sacrament of marriage. This is beauty in its purest form. This union of the lower with the higher is the beautifying of the temple of the body, fitting it for occupation by the Lord. When Jesus said: 'That except a man be born again, he cannot see the Kingdom of God', He was referring to this mystical union of male and female. The last barrier preventing the soul from taking control over the triple entity has now gone down.

"There, good brother, is a nut-shell version of the esoteric value of sex; which may be vaster and more embracing than most people realise.

"Does it help you to see what happens, when you remove sex from its place beside work and play? Do you realise how man has crippled, misled and delayed the master-plan because, instead of regarding the female as his equal, he has eternally tried to subdue her?

"This Chauvinist caper originated in the East, and it has unfortunately seduced the West as well.

"But man and woman remain equal in the eyes of God. Both, in short, have always been equal.

"The final issue I wish to discuss is the mortal attitude towards death. If you will recall my simile of the ageing car, whose original function had been to move you from one place to another, I saw nothing inhuman or callous in your decision to retire it and get a new one. Will you concede that this logic applies equally to death? It does to us on these golden planes; which is why I suggest that it is equally true of you in the mortal shell you now inhabit.

"When I first got here, it took me a long time to get used to what I mistook for callousness — the unimportance these wonderfully loving souls attach to mortal death. The cataclysms and catastrophies which happen on your earth are regarded here with complete equanimity. When a volcano blows itself to pieces, or a typhoon causes a hundred thousand souls to reassemble here at this astral level, there is no weeping or wailing or gnashing of teeth.

"There *is* a touch of mild frustration at the life-spans wasted. The souls concerned will have to be given new bodies and sent back to your material plane. But it causes inconvenience, nothing more. We never indulge the luxury of deep mourning which so hypnotises the bereaved on earth.

"Always look at death straight in the eye, good brother. Recognise the common sense of it. To us, the body is simply an expendable vehicle. When it wears out, we scrap it and rent a new one. When it has been too seriously damaged, we throw it away and requisition a sound one. The only negative factor is the delay the individual suffers while he learns from scratch how to use his new body.

"Forget the cruel and senseless loss involved — unless you only mourn because you feel you're rather hard done by, now that the apple of your eye will no longer gladden your leisure?

"Think on this, good brother. It may seem hard and calculating, but it *is* a fact. When I was catapulted into this world, you sent me love. You sent me power and strength. You wished me well in my new environment. This is as it should be. *There should always be such wishes for a safe arrival.*

"When a ship leaves harbour, you wave the passengers godspeed and a happy voyage. When the ship reaches its destination, the crowd there welcomes it with great delight. Death follows exactly the same procedure.

"Never weep for *yourself*, good brother. For when you grieve for those who have gone ahead of you, you *are* only grieving for yourself. The sugar with which I coat the pill is the fact that what I say is perfectly true. You may not be able to be *happy* about death, but it will cost far less in wear and tear to be honest. So look at it without wearing blinkers!

"And so this little homily comes to its close. We have been

100

able to converse about my new world and my new self, and I look to you to bring our 'rap sessions' to the attention of your mortal brothers. Truth is like a yeast. It needs to come in contact with a receptive ear before it can ferment and become digestible.

"There are many hundreds of thousands of ordinary young people today who seek spiritual counsel, and they have very little to guide them. May this book point to a valid sign post: every reader must still walk the path himself.

"I send the warmest blessings to you from these golden planes. To those of you who still have work to do in the confines of the earth, do not be heavy of heart. Ahead of you my brothers, lies only light and happiness. Your labours will be rewarded by the love, the warmth and the comfort of the Eternal Father of us all.

"The most urgent message that I wished to communicate to you, good brother, was that death has no terror. If no more than *one* of this book's readers accepts that truth, you and I have discharged the duty laid upon us both.

"May His blessing be with you all, now and evermore.

"From the depths of His great heart, His love eternal enfolds each and every one of us."

Other recommended reading . . .

THE SPIRITUAL TEACHINGS OF WHITE EAGLE

AND THEIR APPLICATIONS IN DAILY LIFE

Ingrid Lind. The White Eagle Lodge is among the most influential of the spiritual groups operating in Britain today and its teachings have been carried to many other parts of the world. Ingrid Lind here provides a concise and informed introduction to the history, development and work of the Lodge.

She tells the remarkable story of how, over fifty years ago, the medium Grace Cooke — also known as Minesta — became the mouthpiece through which the message of the spiritual teacher White Eagle was conveyed to the world and how the organization she then helped to found developed as a means of channelling the Christ Light.

The role of the Lodge in recent years is described in detail, and the reader is directed to sources of further information on such subjects as the Five Great Laws, healing and meditation — all of them cornerstones of White Eagle's teaching. She also deals with opportunities in the Lodge for service through sending out the Light and the Lodge's approach to yoga and the study of the zodiac, as well as to the part played by children in the movement.

CHANNELING

INVESTIGATIONS ON RECEIVING INFORMATION FROM PARANORMAL SOURCES

Jon Klimo. Who are Seth, Lazaris, Michael, the Space Brothers, and Ramtha?

They are all channeled entities, personalities who claim to come from somewhere outside our normal consensus reality — through people among us. Their purpose, they say, is to help humanity grow and mature.

Jon Klimo investigates contacts from paranormal sources throughout history:

- who has been contacted?
- what is the content of the messages?
- why is there a startling uniformity among the messages?
- how might this phenomenon be explained — psychological disturbance, telepathy, or are they in fact beings from another dimension?
- how can you make sound judgements as to the validity of channeling?
- what is the significance of channeling for society as a whole and for each of us individually?
- do you have potential to become a vehicle for a channeled entity?

A SOUL'S JOURNEY

Peter Richelieu. While in a state of despair, after the death of his brother, the author is visited by Acharya, an Indian mystic. Using astral projection, Acharya takes him out of the physical world onto the astral planes of the 'afterlife'. Each astral plane teaches the author something new about life and death, karma and the ego. Through a series of meetings with the 'dead' — including his brother — the author comes to realize how irrational it is to fear death.

Through his teaching, Acharya opens up a whole new vision of life in the world that follows this, a world where anything is possible.

Based on notes taken immediately following out-of-body experiences, this book is both enlightening and absorbing. It leaves the reader feeling he too has had a direct insight into the unknown mysteries of life and death.